The Daily Skeptic
A Collection of Essays from 2016

The Daily Skeptic:
A Collection of Essays from 2016

Cody Scott

Cody Scott: The Daily Skeptic Blog
2017

First Printing: January 2017

ISBN 978-1-365-61987-8

The Daily Skeptic Blog
519 E Hospital Street
Nacogdoches, TX 75961

www.dailyskepticblog.wordpress.com

Dedication

To my beautiful wife and best friend, Olivia, without her, I would not have had the support to start writing

Contents

Introduction

Being a news junkie myself, I decided to jump on the bandwagon and start my own blog. But being a Skeptic, I plan to use my blog for good. I will start to post news articles from a skeptical and investigated angle. I despise the biased news, and usually end up researching stories, so why not create a blog to flex my writing abilities as well?

I plan to work this blog daily, mainly writing about a news article a day.

Monday – Thursday I will post daily news ranging from politics, health, science (pseudoscience), business, and historical stories. I want Friday to be Good Friday where I post on stories related to religion, science, philosophy and the like. Saturday will be a week in review were I will either review the direction of the news stories or touch on a story that seems important enough to warrant another article.

And finally, Sunday will be my book review day where I will touch on books I loved or hated.

August 10, 2016

That was the original post I made about my blog. Of course, many things changed. I've started new jobs, started a career, had my first child, and got distracted since then. Yes, the blog originally was made to investigate news and share my findings. The blog, I hope, stayed true to the "skeptic" mentality – I still wrote about global events, but branched into bogus claims and false news articles (of which there is no shortage of), and I also began to cover books, people, and other materials that brought more meat to the blog.

Throughout the end of 2016, I covered the numerous global events as well as the election and the election fallout. I hope that this book will be a testament to the infamous "2016" as well as the start of this new hobby of mine.

August 2016

The Confirmation Bias: Our Enemy

Once you notice it, you cannot un-notice it. It is absolutely necessary to decisions, opinions, and actions, and yet, it is missing from the majority of today's conversations. And that is critical thinking - the ability to think before believing and asserting. Far too often than we would like to admit, we jump to conclusions. Since childhood, we are told think and we accept them as facts. It's only natural since such beliefs are drilled into our evolutionary survival. A parent tells their child to stay away from the lion's den because it is dangerous. If every child has to go investigate every claim, there will be no more children! They would all be dead. These are our ancestors. And although it is useful for survival, we must break away from this primitive and childish way of thinking.

It does not have to be a parent advising a child. The vast majority of beliefs held today are political or religious or both! Let's say I am a conservative youngster just beginning to look into the world of politics. I stumble across and article (conservative) that says Global Warming isn't real. Because I self-identify as a conservative, I would accept that as fact! Who has the time to research it? And since I know it is from a conservative source, I defiantly wouldn't investigate, because it already confirms my belief. There is a lot of evidence that people seem to migrate to their own beliefs and read only sources that confirms their opinions. Imagine the relief they get when religious devotees are falling away from the church and attend service. They are over whelmed and no doubt relieved to see that so many people agree with their beliefs. One can easily see how this confirmation bias would work for the mentally insane – how overwhelmingly pleased they are when they find others to believe in their irrational yet convincing ideals. This bias, officially called the "Confirmation Bias" is well researched, but is not well communicated.

"If one were to attempt to identify a single problematic aspect of human reasoning that deserves attention above all others, the confirmation bias would have to be among the candidates for consideration. Many have written about this bias, and it appears to be sufficiently strong and pervasive that one is led to wonder whether the bias, by itself, might account for a significant fraction of the disputes, altercations, and misunderstandings that occur among individuals, groups, and nations."– R. Nickerson

Of course people know about it, but what does it have to do with them? Of course they are right. But I strongly believe that everyone falls victim to this dreadful bias. I have plenty of times! Remember that poor Conservative youngster from above? That was me! It took many years of stubborn fact searching but I finally became aware of it. I defiantly do not think I have it all figured out, but it is what we don't know that makes people intelligent. I think the late Christopher Hitchens puts it best: "The essence of the independent mind lies not in what it thinks, but in how it thinks"

August 11, 2016

Mike Pence the Credulous

More like Mike the non-thinker. In a recent News interview with MSNBC, the Republican Vice Presidential Nominee, believes "Evolution is just a theory". And just when I thought the Republican ticket may have a candidate with some brains, Pence decided to throw away any intellectual vote. Beyond the brain rot I could go on about, this really goes to show the voter the thought process behind the candidates. (1)

In fact, the Evolution vs Intelligent Design debate is perfect to quickly determine people's thought process; that is, one's opinion on the matter can greatly assist in determining if that person is a critical thinker. I challenge the reader to use this tool to decide if the person has some capability of critical thought. (2)

The truth is it always was a theory, Mr. Speaker. And now that we have recognized evolution as a theory, I would simply and humbly ask, can we teach it as such and can we also consider teaching other theories of the origin of species? Like the theory that was believed in by every signer of the Declaration of Independence. Every signer of the Declaration of Independence believed that men and women were created and were endowed by that same Creator with certain unalienable rights. The Bible tells us that God created man in his own imagine, male and female. He created them. And I believe that, Mr. Speaker

First, Pence needs to know that a "theory" in scientific terms is difference than just a hypothesis. Second, there is no creditable, verifiable alternative to evolution. Third, not every signer of the Declaration of Independence or Founding Father believed in a higher power (like Thomas Jefferson, Benjamin Franklin, Cornett Harnett, John Adams, James Madison, and Alexander Hamilton to name a few) (3)

I appeal to the fair mindedness of the readers and assume you believe in evolution. the basis for its "belief" is founded in fact. Any critic who says otherwise has no viable alternative except the old "POOF! God did it with magic!" We have to grow out of this.

And just as we expect a certain rational analysis in our own thought, we defiantly need it in our presidential candidates. I challenge the reader to use the Evolution VS Creation tool to determine between a fact and credulity.

August 11, 2016

Glenn Beck is Called Out

Glenn Beck, a hub for free thought without the "thought" part, accused a man for a part in the Boston bombing earlier this week, but how can he make this accusation? Could it be that he has knowledge unknown to the government or its people? Of course not. This is yet another example of his belief system. His credulous beliefs are usually benign or just silly (remember when he fasted for Ted Cruz to win the Republican candidacy?), but this has taken a dangerous step.

Recently, he has been becoming less and less popular due to his air headed remarks during the last campaign, but Beck seems to need some sort of attention. It is far too easy to imagine him as a toddler, fighting for attention. but the accusation is a step too far and it has been noticed.

The weeks following the attack, Beck alleged that the government had labeled 20-year-old Abdulrahman Alharbi as a "proven terrorist" who funded the operation.

"You know who the Saudi is?" Beck, formerly of Fox News, said. "He's the guy who paid for it."

The claim was untrue, unfair, and irresponsible. Alharbi was questioned, his home searched and cleared by the authorities. But people are catching on! U.S. District Judge Patti B. Saris, has demanded proof from Beck. Finally! Justice! It is doubtful that he can provide that proof because he doesn't deal in proof. Of course Beck has good ideals involving personal freedoms, but evidence is not his specialty.

If Beck fails to produce evidence, the judge threatens to jail Beck for contempt. To be fair, Beck should also be tried for slander.

August 12, 2016

Closet Sexists

In my daily life, I was surprised to find myself in a room full of adults declaring women cannot hold political office. I was astounded! It really makes one think of what they think about the women around them, or indeed themselves (as some were women themselves). But It turns out, that these closet sexists are far more wide spread than one would expect from a western country in the year 2016.

The most recent case, and the reason I was drawn to write about this, is Bryan Fischer comment. If you don't know who he is, it's because you probably have an IQ over 80. This old charlatan relies on the Bronze Aged morals to run his, and everyone else's lives - including not allowing women into a high political office. Here is the clip if you need a dose of brain-rot (1)

"I don't think women should be entrusted with high political office... you could make a good Biblical case"

Fischer may not be able to use them, but he has the balls to even go after Massachusetts Judge Debra McCloskey Todd. And this is where the brainless sexists really get it messed up. Debra Todd is extremely suitable to be Judge. She has been serving since the eighties and has an extensive list of achievements that qualify her for office. (Here is the list http://www.pacourts.us/courts/supreme-court/supreme-court-justices/justice-debra-mccloskey-todd)

And yet, this is meaningless to this old prune. His mind is stuck in 2000 B.C. Jerusalem. The same with all the other supposed adults who hold this to heart. They may even think it is moral to keep women out of high office. This is just another tool you can use to truly judge someone's mental capabilities, for these people truly belong in the infancy of our species.

August 13, 2016

The 5000 Year Leap Backwards [Book Review]

Cleon Skousen wrote *The 5000 Year Leap* in 1981 slightly predating the Conservative reformation and it shows. Slightly eager to read a book summarizing the American Ideals of freedom, I picked up the book after it sat on my bookshelf for a few years. There was not even a crease in the spin before I was let down. Any Neo-con or Reagan – Era conservative may have already interpreted me as a freedom hating liberal, but please read on. If you are a true lover of freedom, you will read on and see the seemingly blatant misinformation the author communicates for his agenda. Skousen as well as the institution that published this book (The National Center for Constitutional Studies) does us a favor by summarizing the basics of freedom, but the reader must keep in mind that although the 1980's Conservative movement was inspired by the global fight for freedom, it is also inspired by the biggest enemy of freedom: Theocracy.

Conveniently for me, *The 5000 Year Leap* draws out exactly what I mean to illustrate by consistently confusing Freedom for Theocracy and Democracy for Totalitarianism. , Thomas Jefferson, aiming to create a more secular and moral Bible, edited it by taking out any miracles or divinity that cannot be proven or explained. I aim to do the same service to The 5000 Year Leap by highlighting the brilliant research of the Founding Fathers, while stressing the blatant misinformation that seems to fester and infect to this day, the Neo-Conservative movement. I hope that my true feelings about liberty is not overwhelmed by my criticisms of it's self-proclaimed protectors. Freedom and Liberty is what the human race has driven for hundreds of thousands of years. It is the perfection of human government and it deserves our respect for that reason. And yet, tragically, I know people will misconstrue my opinions of this book because I am criticizing it's authors. But in order to obtain the truth, especially on such important matters, we must be skeptical.

Skousen spares no time revealing his book as well as the publisher's agenda within the first six pages. He immediately admits he thinks the founding of America was "guided and governed by the hand of god" (page 1). But then continues to list brilliant quotes by our founding fathers, all of whom are agnostics. Among those quoted: James Madison, John Adams, Benjamin Franklin, George Washington, Alexander Hamilton, and Thomas Jefferson are all agnostic, secular leaders without whom, we could not have had such a perfect and universal constitution. Part of the Treaty of Tripoli was ratified by Congress in 1791 without debate clearly stated: *'The government of the United States of America is not in any sense founded on the Christian religion.'*

"When all men of all religions shall enjoy equal liberty, property, and an equal chance for honors and power we may expect that improvements will be made in the human character and the state of society" –John Adams

I contemplate with sovereign reverence that act of the whole American people which declared that their legislature should make no law respecting an establishment of religion, or prohibit the free exercise thereof, thus building a wall of separation between church and state – Thomas Jefferson

Christianity neither is, nor ever was a part of the common law – Thomas Jefferson

Strongly guarded as is the separation between Religion and Government in the Constitution of the United States, the danger of encroachment by Ecclesiastical Bodies, may be illustrated by precedents already furnished in their short history – James Madison

This basic belief that our Founding Fathers created the constitution with spiritual influence is what corrupts the Neo-Conservative movement in a big way. Conservatives, the protectors of liberty and freedom, have the thorn of religion in their side; one that has become more painful as the country moves away from a spiritually lead country to a secular one.

It cannot be ignored that nothing about god is included in the constitution and it shouldn't. And yet one cannot have a serious conversation about liberty without stumbling on the idea that god gave us this freedom. The author seems to think that such a universal document could not be conjured up without religion, but it leaves the rational reader to wonder "why would god wait until the 18th century to guide this sort of country?" It is the sort of thought that poisons any sort of serious conversation about our constitution. Have no mistake: this is not a harmless belief. Peter Marshall illustrates this point perfectly in the forward when he admits, "The choice before us is plain: Christ or chaos, conviction or compromise, discipline or disintegration. I am rather tired of hearing about our rights and privileges as American citizens...America's future depends upon her accepting and demonstration God's government" Would a quote like this be out of place in a radical Muslim country? The point of this quote perfectly sets up the bias for the reader: Freedom is an inalienable right...But you must submit to god (and the right god). This comes before everything else, especially the "rights and privileges" of American citizens. Ronald Mann, contributor, also attributes our biggest threats to liberty is because Americans have, "evicted 'Providence' from our counsels, schools, courts, and assemblies" (page xvii). Again, I must ask: would this quote be out of place in Iran or even North Korea? Granted, North Korea is not a religious state, but it possesses the same qualities that the author mistakes for liberty. If we are to hold the purest for of liberty, we must examine these claims.

Put bluntly: *"Religion is a totalitarian belief. It is the wish to be a slave. It is the desire that there be an unalterable, unchallengeable, tyrannical authority who can convict you of thought crime while you are asleep, who can subject you to total surveillance around the clock every waking and sleeping minute of your life, before you're born and, even worse and where the real fun begins, after you're dead; a celestial North Korea. Who wants this to be true? Who but a slave desires such a ghastly fate? I've been to North Korea. It has a dead man as its president, Kim Jong-Il is only head of the party and head of the army. He's not head of the state. That office belongs to his deceased father, Kim Il-Sung. It's a necrocracy, a thanatocracy. It's one short of a trinity I might add. The son is the reincarnation of the father. It is the most revolting and utter and absolute and heartless tyranny the human species has ever evolved. But at least you can fucking die and leave North Korea!"* (1) – Christopher Hitchens

It is important to understand their key points about Ruler's Law versus the People's rule of law. This is an extremely well organized way to lay out Tyranny versus Democracy. However well put together, it is laughably ironic how quickly the author contradicts himself here. In this section, Skousen lists the following as Ruler's Law:

- Authority under Ruler's Law is nearly always established by, force, violence, and conquest
- All sovereign power is considered to be in the conqueror or his descendants
- People are not equal, but divided by classes
- The entire country is considered to be the property o the ruler. He speaks of it as his 'realm'
- The thrust of governmental power is from the top down...
- The people have no unalienable rights

And so on.

Quickly, flip the page and read about where the Founding Father's first found the common law of freedom: Ancient Israel. Now, one can already see that the author has no idea what he is talking about. Please take the above and flip to a random page in Deuteronomy, and it will fit perfectly with the above Ruler's Law. The confidence in the author's knowledge should make anyone in the church embarrassed when he explains how Moses established freedom and liberty in Deuteronomy. This book, along with the Ten Commandments completely aligns themselves with the Ruler's Law (The very first three commandments are orders to worship the dear leader and only the dear leader). Deuteronomy is the book that claims to be the foundation of freedom and liberty and yet the author admits the kingdom of Israel failed to live up to its freedom principles when they adopted slaves. Skousen fails to mention that the books of Deuteronomy lays out that the Jews could own slaves and even sets rules about how to keep them. It would be difficult to find a more profound example of misinformation...Until you get to the next page (page 16) when he says Moses was the leader of Israel. The Bible clearly says that Moses was never allowed to enter into the kingdom of Israel.

The reader gets some relief as they enter the 28 Principles of freedom, but one should not get too comfortable. The painstakingly made stretch the author attempts to connect religion and liberty continues when you get to the second principle. The author makes very large claims by saying the Founding Fathers get the idea of freedom and love form his common man from the Ten Commandments. One does not need to point out the first three commandments are completely irrelevant for freedom, not to mention morality; but the claim that the Golden Rule is somewhere within the Ten Commandments complete discredits the author's knowledge of the word. The Golden Rule, although not in the Old Testament what so ever, has been around long since Bronze Aged Israel. The oldest is recorded in Ancient Babylonia from an unknown author and even recorded by Confucius. Could this mean that humans are competent enough to run a libertarian, free government without the assistance of a divine being? Skousen says no, and attempts to wrestle the Founding Fathers into this idea as well. In Article 3 of the Northwest ordinance (if you haven't heard of it, that's because it has little bearing on modern day), Congress has said, "Religion, morality, and knowledge being necessary to good government and the happiness of mankind, schools and the means of education shall forever be encouraged." Although later, the author admits that the

Founding Fathers desire a separation between church and state, he now declares that Congress and the Founding Fathers are in favor of teaching religion in schools.

Also note how the author has complete disregard for the people's opinions. It is a symptom of the religious power that infects Conservatives ability to truly protect people's rights. The author tries to explain how time and time again, the people vote for the 'wrong' people or we are going down the wrong path. Perhaps Skousen separates Democracy, and freedom. It is unfathomable to mistake Theocracy for Liberty, and yet this book unashamedly asserts this throughout the book.

August 14, 2016

The Forgotten Holy War

It has been a little over 2 years since it started. It is forgotten in the news and so unheard of – I even forgot about it! It is the Saudi Arabian war against the new Yemen government.

The public strive was apparent as far back as 2012 when former President Ali Abdullah Saleh resigned following the Arab Spring protests. Since then, Yemen has been in a sort of "civil war" between government forces and the "Houthis"; a Shiite Muslim rebel force trying to take control of the country.

The Saudi Arabian government, as well as the rest of the world believes there has been an Iranian and Iraqi influence in the area that used to be Saudi. Whether or not that is completely true remains to be seen. Either way, the Saudis are fighting for control of their little corner of the Middle East by sending 150,000 troops into Yemen to "stabilize" the region. Saudi Arabian representatives have described this intervention as and effort toward, "security and stability through establishing a political process". Because of this goal, the Western War seem to have ignored the war.

Why bring up this war now? Besides its lack of attention, and obvious religious aggression; there has been a deadly air strike on a militia camp in Yemen over the weekend. The shocking part was that the militia camp was not a militia camp – it was a school full of children ages ranging from 6 to 8 years old. This has finally caught global attention!

UNICEF's Jean Harneis said Sunday, "We've had a verification team who went to the site and was there on the day. We've been to the hospital and we've spoken to parents. Many of these children were six-years old, eight-years old. There's just no way that those were fighters". The most recent count is 28 injured and 10 dead. UNICEF took the publicity and erroneously exclaimed that another 100,000 children will die from lack of resources they would have had if it weren't for the war. How they got that number, I don't know. But what is sure is that this is nothing less than a Holy War. Had those children been Saudi, perhaps there would have been more care when initiating an air strike. I am doubtful the world community will do much to intervene in this conflict maybe they shouldn't. But at least we can take this war for what it is: a century old Holy War.

August 15, 2016

Student Loan Forgiveness

The idea of forgiving all student loans is back in the news with pressure from presidential candidate Jill Stein along with special interest groups like Signon.org and Moveon.org – but is it a good idea?

There is no doubt I feel their pain. I have recently graduated college (a degree in Accounting of all things) and could not find a job. So I ended up going into huge debt for literally nothing! Maybe bragging rights – since an accounting degree is so cool.

The horrible job market is the direct cause of the jobless college grads. Companies can't hire as many people, so they might as well hire someone more experienced with more degrees. And out of this frustration comes over 300,000 signatures for the issue and a presidential candidate. But what would happen if all student loans were forgiven?

On their website, Signon claims:

Forgiving the student loan debt of all Americans will have an immediate simulative effect on our economy. With the stroke of the President's pen, millions of Americans would suddenly have hundreds, or in some cases, thousands of extra dollars in their pockets each and every month with which to spend on ailing sectors of the economy. As consumer spending increases, businesses will begin to hire, jobs will be created and a new era of innovation, entrepreneurship and prosperity will be ushered in for all.

The evidence for this claim is nonexistent. Of course, the health of the economy depends on college grads getting into the workforce. But arbitrarily forgiving debt is not the way to do that. For one, no debt does NOT mean there will be more jobs - there is no correlation what so ever. I want to remind the reader I would LOVE being debt free – but anyone with a college education should realize it is not feasible.

Many people have already investigated the possibility of forgiving student debt and there is a strong consensus that it is a bad idea. Forgiving student loans would not stop future loans from being made. The president does not have the power to forgive student loans. With the loan companies stay stable if they know the government will simply forgive debt?

What is really needed is a cool-headed response to the crisis. We need to realize, even if we are in debt, the loans clearly gave terms that were agreed to. We need to understand that forgiving debt will not create jobs. And finally, if someone like Jill Stein was in power to forgive debt, there is no way responsible congressman would allow that to happen. With all the debt in America today, no special interest group would allow this write off without their own considered.

Reasons why Student Debt write-off would NOT work:

1. No debt does NOT mean employment.

2. The president does NOT have that power

3. Student loan terms are clearly defined and are easy on your wallet

4. Forgiving student loans would destabilize the loan companies. They would not easily lend to future students there for, future students will have difficulty getting loans

5. Loan forgiveness is NOT stimulating. Simulating the economy needs spending money

6. Why college grads? Aren't they the ones most likely to get a job?

If there is anyone who thinks this is actually a good idea after investigating the claims, obviously doesn't have or deserve a college education.

I refer the level-headed reader to Representative Karen Bass's page regarding the Student Loan Fairness act where a bipartisan bill is in the works to control interest rates as well as stress financial responsibility while providing a safety net to those who are struggling to pay. (1)

August 16, 2016

Turkish Witch Hunt

After the failed coup in Turkey, there have been demands for the U.S. to release cleric Fethullah Gulen. Gulen is a self-banished cleric now living in Pennsylvania who is now being blamed for the Turkish coup that has turned into a Turkish Kristallnacht. People belonging to Gulen's movement are being hunted down in the streets. One anonymous member described it like being a Jew in Germany.

Fethullah Gulen's movement is called Hizmet (or *"the service"*) and members are called Cemaat (*"the community"*). They are an international Islamic movement that was once an ally to the Turkish government. There is little information about their platform or goals except that they are "cult-like" and secretive in its membership and ideals. The Turkish government, led by the Justice and Development Party, usually tries to lean towards a secular government. A pleasant thing to see in the region! But regardless of Hizmet's denial of the involvement in the coup, the once secular Turkish government is now shutting them down. Their main attacks have been Hizmet schools and communities.

The tension between the group and the government began a few years ago when Prime Minister Recep Tayyip Erdoğan ran into a power struggle with Gulan when antigovernment rhetoric was suspected. In response, the government shutdown many Hizmet pre-university schools. In the first step toward even more trouble Gulan responded,

"If I were to say anything to people I may say people should vote for those who are respectful to democracy, rule of law, who get on well with people. Telling or encouraging people to vote for a party would be an insult to people's' intellect. Everybody very clearly sees what is going on."

The fateful comment eventually led to the self-banishment of the leader. Although this has yet to be clear evidence of the coup link, it does seem that the government is scared for its life and it's power. It is a back and forth cat fight between cleric and tyrant that has turned deadly.

As the witch hunt continues, one has to wonder if this is still secular government we knew in the region and what exactly the West will think about this loss of Democracy.

August 17, 2016

Exaggeration and Ukraine do not Mix

Fear mounts as the NATO allies (including the US) and Russia are moving more troops to the Ukraine border. Earlier today, Putin stations over 40,000 troops on the Ukraine border threatening the yearlong lull in the conflict. This may or may not be a reaction to the U.S. fulfilling its commitment to assisting the NATO forces in the eastern front by sending its own troops. This is another push to "World War III" – but is that a rational conclusion, or a drastic over exaggeration?

You may notice, when a big event occurs be it a technological advancement, a political change, or even a UFO, we see stories all the time that point to the biggest conclusion. I bet the reader has already thought of some examples.

Over exaggerations are completely normal human traits – however irrational. The erg to over exaggerate stories is a way we get people's attention or a way of storytelling itself. But the human Psyche may offer a clearer picture as to why people just to the biggest conclusions. The Psychological Journal 'Emotion' published a study in which the test subjects would or would not over exaggerate. The researchers checked their vitals and noticed the ones over exaggerating were overwhelmingly more calm and confident. The reason, Dr. Gramzow determined, "It's basically an exercise in projecting the self toward one's goals".

It would also seem that over exaggeration, though useful in the media, helps spread stories and gather attention. Because it is an irrational reaction, it needs to be carefully examined. One needs to be skeptical.

Of course military moves by Putin and other world leaders need to be taken seriously – but with a grain of salt. Same with UFO sightings or government conspiracies, extreme claims require extreme evidence, and assuming this means World War III, is silly. Let us handle the situation as is to avoid any rash or impulsive decisions.

August 18, 2016

Martin Luther King Jr – and the Death Penalty

In 1998, James Earl Ray is reduced to a dying puddle of filth only reflecting his life of hate and bigotry. Thanks to Hepatitis C, Mr. Ray died (finally) at the age of 70 to kidney disease and liver failure; a fitting death for such a murderer but one can't help but to think there should be something more deserving of this beer stained barbarian.

As most know, Ray was responsible for assassinating Martin Luther King Jr. back in 1968 with one all-encompassing rifle shot with which Ray stole a public figure from us. We can't begin to imagine what this felon stole from us by killing Martin Luther King, but it seems all too easy for us to imagine what kind of punishment may be fitting for such a toad of a man. If one gets to know me, they would know my slight bias toward using the death penalty for the most extreme cases and with that said and with the context of my essay must force the reader to wonder: could the death penalty been used against Mr. Ray?

Recall the capital punishment ban movement throughout the 1960's and through the 70's lowered the number of criminals put to death to zero in most years. Could this movement be the reason for not only keeping Ray alive and also providing a death free out come to committing the assassination? The death penalty, though not proved, has a stigma of being a deterrent to serious crimes. Before Ray shot Mr. King, there had been a few years of anti-death penalty ideals that could very well have lead many people to the idea of committing heinous crimes and assassinating Mr. King.

Whether or not that makes one think, we have to accordingly apply this idea to the opposite way. Did the assassination of Martin Luther King Jr. finally strike the general population so intensely that they reconsidered capital punishment as a viable punishment? This could be an even stronger point to make when talking about the assassination's influence with capital punishment. If MLK's death made the death penalty an option again, then maybe we owe him more than we give him credit for. Not only was he the biggest speaker for equality in his time, but also for civil and criminal justice!

The lesson, if my wondering thoughts have made any connections to the reader, is that the decisions and public movements have a much bigger influence toward national events. Huge and radical events maybe a result of any rash and emotional movements and to jump at and cling to such movements have shown to be naïve and foolish.

August 20, 2016

Nuclear Energy Misinformation

I must be either optimistic, naive or both. The battle against misinformation regarding Nuclear Power is still raging – and its raging in some unsuspecting places. I usually wouldn't write about this since it seems like a no-brainer. I felt compelled to touch on the major points regarding Nuclear Energy in response to some brain rot that is circling the internet.

Jill Stein, the Green Party presidential candidate, recently tweeted:

"Nuclear power plants = weapons of mass destruction waiting to be detonated. Time to shut them down" (1)

After a clear lack of any economic skills, I doubted Jill Stein understands of the issues. But now that she has spoken on Nuclear Energy – it is clear Stein lacks a basic understanding of the energy, scientific, and political facts. The fact that she really thinks a nuclear power plant is a weapon would be humorous, if not for her following. If she does not even know that, how can any reasonable person still support her? Thankfully, she isn't doing so well.

First of all, Nuclear Energy is already providing about 20% of America's energy. It is doing even more wonders in Europe because it provides huge amounts of energy for an incredibly low price (compared to coal and especially when compared to solar), and with no environmental impact.

Second, it is safe energy! Especially when compared to fossil fuels. There have only been 3 disasters with nuclear energy ever (3 mile island included, but it really shouldn't be) whereas with fossil fuels there were 10 in the past 25 years (2).

So safe, most scientists are pro-nuclear! Sunniva Rose asks, *"How is it possible to worry about global warming, and not be pro-nuclear?" (3)*. A good question for the misinformed Green Party. And finally, you cannot make weapons from a nuclear power plant. This part is a little confusing if one hasn't researched this. The materials used in a power plant (Plutonium) can be made into a weapon, but the plant itself cannot explode or be converted into a weapon (4).

It is a pretty silly scare tactic used by environmentalists – but these scare tactics MUST be investigated – especially if it means losing an amazing power source like nuclear energy. This is a perfect power source! A miracle of modern science! It provides clean long-lasting energy (which should appeal to the Left) and it produces huge amounts of energy at a price lower than fossil fuels (which should appeal to the Right). And yet, we are still arguing about it! Before picking a side – please investigate it yourself. I will provide sources below

August 20, 2016

US Science and Math Scores on the Rise

Finally! The United States students have scored better in mathematics and science! The National Assessment of Educational Progress has been following American students throughout the 1990's and 2000's and have found dramatic increases in the US's math and science scores – and that's good news internationally.

NAEP rated only 42% of fourth graders and 36% of eighth graders "proficient" or "advanced" in math up from 17% and 26% in 1990. There has also been a steady rise in science scores as well, but they do see to level out within the most recent years. These overall trends shows a very bright future, but I cannot write an honest report on this without mentioning in 2013, scores have dropped internationally since 1990. But, although worrying, should bring international attention.

Science is the product of human ingenuity, intelligence, and collective progress. The more we know about the world around us, the more people can respect and care for each other to bring further progress. It was the late Carl Sagan who said

It has been said that astronomy is a humbling and character-building experience. There is perhaps no better demonstration of the folly of human conceits than this distant image of our tiny world. To me, it underscores our responsibility to deal more kindly with one another, and to preserve and cherish the pale blue dot, the only home we've ever known.

The obvious, yet slipping US grip on the title "super power" can be a good thing to the international community – but only if we can return our interests back to scientific learning. It was the scientifically minded who modernize health and medicine, created energy to fuel our world, and land a man on the moon. It has been the ignorant and arrogant regressive who shun and deny scientific findings – which, as throughout history – has always been the case.

There has always been an infant-like fear of science that has kept progress from continuing forward (Poor Galileo). And those people are alive and well today, but thanks to scientific interests, and popular scientists taking a stand, the regressive are losing. And when they lose, we all win.

August 23, 2016

Target Bows to Demands – It's still not Enough

The Target fiasco has been drawn out with embarrassing Target videos of people yelling at Target employees. It all started when Target took a seemingly harmless and common sense action to make their stores more comfortable for their Trans-Gender customers. It was met by the most brutal and unnecessary protests of their stores. In recent days, the Target bathroom policy seems to have died down... Until now!

The main force against Target is the American Family Association, whose boycott of Target is still active. Wanting to find common ground, Target asked for a solution. The American Family Association demands are:

One solution is a common-sense approach and a reasonable solution to the issue of transgendered customers: a unisex bathroom. Target should keep separate facilities for men and women, but for the trans community and for those who simply like using the bathroom alone, a single occupancy unisex option should be provided.

Installing private bathrooms would cost Target $20 Million to complete...but guess what? They Agreed! Yes! Target is hoping to put this bathroom issue behind them by installing private bathrooms – a multimillion dollar program to make everyone happy and comfortable. Even though Target met 100% of the American Family Association, they still don't accept it!

The afternoon following the peace deal, The American Family Association sent out an email stating:

Last week, Target announced a $20 million public relations diversionary tactic to make you believe the company has changed its bathroom policy. Don't fall for it. Target has not changed its policy. While it is true the company is adding single-stall, lockable bathrooms to all store locations, Target says it will continue to allow men to use women's restrooms and fitting rooms inside their stores

As if the regressive didn't sound illogical enough, we – and Target – now know when they make any demands, they don't mean them. Target, however, has yet again taken the high ground and is simply trying to make their customers more comfortable. Remember this when The American Family Association demand anything: they cannot be trusted.

August 23, 2016

Glenn Beck Called Out [Update]

I published a post last week about Glenn Beck accusing a man cleared by the government of funding the Boston Bombing. He alleged that the government had labeled 20-year-old Abdulrahman Alharbi as a "proven terrorist" who funded the operation. As Skeptical as I hope the reader is, one must ask "how does he know this fact that has eluded government officials and media outlets?" That's a good question and one's assumption will prove correct: He has no idea what he is talking about.

Thankfully, U.S. District Judge Patti B. Saris is just as skeptical and demanded Glenn Beck to provide proof or for him to reveal his source. This demand is reasonable. If Beck's assertion is correct, then Abdulrahman Alharbi can be brought to justice – if the assertion is a blatant lie, Beck can be found to be in contempt of the court.

To be honest, Glenn Becks irresponsible cry for attention should really be charged for sander and or libel against Alharbi. And today, Glenn Beck finally responded to the court saying they "were unwilling to be identified," even though Judge Saris said she would keep their names out of the record. Now why, if Beck is so set on the fact that Alharbi is a terrorist-funding criminal, wouldn't he comply? Doesn't he want this suspected terrorist in jail?

Of course he doesn't because he knows Alharbi is innocent. Beck needs nothing short of a miracle to bail him out of this lie. Maybe he should start fasting?

August 25, 2016

The Power of Prayer

I have heard a lot about the results of multiple prayer studies. It is well-known that they failed, but I decided to research it myself. Prayers offered by strangers had no effect on the recovery of people – in fact – the study shows that patients are *worse off* for prayers. There have been multiple studies regarding the power of prayer, mainly by the Templeton Foundation, The American Heart Journal, and numerous doctors; most notably Dr. Herbert Benson and Dr. Charles Bethea (1).

The study used over 1800 patients, which – if you are familiar with statistics – is far above the amount necessary to gather results. The final study cost over $2.4 million dollars from religious organizations with additional subsidies from the government. The U.S. government has invested $2.3 million since 2000 (2).

In the study, the patients were divided into three groups – 2 were prayed for and one was not. One of the two prayed for were told they were being prayed for, the other was not aware.

The results shown that

Those who know they were being prayed for suffered more complications after treatment (59% compared to 51%)

Those who were prayed for suffered from more "major complications" than the group that was not prayed for (18% compared to 13%)(3)

It should be noted that the study was largely done with a strong religious bias. Remember, it was funded by the Templeton Foundation (those guys who put Bibles in hotels) and conducted by two Christian doctors working at the Integris Baptist Medical Center in Oklahoma City. All leaders in the study said it was inconclusive.

Dr. Charles Bethea remarked "*One conclusion from this is that the role of awareness of prayer should be studied further*"

Even the doctor from the secular Mayo Clinic said, "*the study said nothing about the power of personal prayer or about prayers for family members and friends*" (1)

With a sample group of over 1800, the difference between the two groups is substantial. One would think the results would be completely clear in favor of the prayer groups. And yet the results are not even equal – it shows that prayer is actually *harmful* in recovery.

There have been numerous studies like this – just not one so thorough and large. Christian groups actually recognize the results but blame those who prayed. Christianity

Today said, "too few patients; unblended researchers or subjects; invalid outcome measures; inappropriate statistical methods; randomization problems; and suspected outright fraud" (5)

Dr. Harold G. Koenig, director of the Center for Spirituality, Theology and Health at the Duke University Medical Center said it right, *"Science is not designed to study the supernatural".* (6)

August 25, 2016

Speaking of Military Coups

There has been a failed coup in Turkey as you know – but do you remember the failed Soviet coup of 1991? Many people don't – and it is the 25th anniversary of the coup!

The Soviet coup was a complete surprise to the US, the western government, as well as the Russians themselves. It all started when Mikhail Gorbachev became general secretary of the Communist Party in 1985 and started to release the Russians from the Soviet grip.

In 1985, the country was economically in the exact same condition it was in 10 years ago in 1975 – no growth and the country could not produce enough goods for its population. Gorbachev most notably started the "Perestroika" which is what the political movement reformation within the Communist party which implemented the Glasnost (meaning "openness") policy giving more market-like freedoms to Russia and its various states (Ukraine, Belarus, etc). Most notable, the act provided more free speech and independent news stations to open the door for more democratic actions.

Come 1989, the Berlin wall suddenly fell with U.S. pressure and further readied Russia for the inevitable political shift. In 1990, Gorbachev actually took huge steps in cutting back on their military budget and lowered the amount of nuclear arms in Soviet possession. He even won a Nobel Peace Prize for that!

All these actions, radical for a Soviet leader, lead to the breakaway of soviet states including Poland, Slovakia, Ukraine and others. Not exactly the reaction Gorbachev expected but he did nothing to stop it and instead attempted to strengthen ties to the new states – which worried the other senior Soviet leaders. The Soviets finally lost their patience when Gorbachev and other leaders drafted a new and freer USSR. It was in August 1991 that the conservative Soviets launched a coup to stop the referendum and restore the old Soviet ways.

Here is where the coup gets really interesting. The Soviet coup was mainly in Moscow and was mostly military forces including tanks. The coup was cut short by local civil resistance. The people actually wanted freedom so much; they went up against the military forces and beat it! Let this be a reminder to all those who attempt a coup against the totalitarian forces of evil. The ingredients for freedom in the face of oppression: people and spirit. The rest will take care of itself.

August 27, 2016

The Epipen Epidemic

I spent a good amount of time honestly trying to find a reason why the lifesaving EpiPen's price was increased so dramatically. I am somewhat versed in business and thought there must be some reason for such an outrageous price increase – I found nothing. It seems that Heather Bresch is the new pharmaceutical villain and – as of now – had no reason for the price increase.

Now, someone who arbitrarily increased a lifesaving drug's price must have a record that at least points to such morals in the past. Heather Bresch is the chief executive of the EpiPen Company, Mylan. Increasing the EpiPen from around $100 to $600 is just scratching the surface. Bresch has a long history of wrong doing and irresponsible business handlings.

Firstly, let no one forget, that Ms. Bresch never got her business degree from West Virginia University – until 10 years after she attended school. She only completed about half of her degrees course work. Why 10 years later? Please don't assume someone like her would go back. She got it back in the same manner she is accustomed to: through dirty dealings. Her father was the state governor Joe Manchin who was able to work things out. The University came out later and revealed that the degree was wrongly awarded.

After her rise to power, her company relocated to the Netherlands to avoid federal taxation. Maybe her ties to the Democratic party tried to stop her. Clinton, after all, is against companies leaving the country to avoid taxation. But the DNC seems to have turned a blind eye.

Her political ties are something to be investigated too. Her father, now a Democratic Representative, keeps her and her company in the loop with the government and even Hillary Clinton. Bresch was able to influence and pass drug laws – even from Europe!

Not only does Bresch owe Americans an explanation, so does Mr. Manchin and leading Democrats. This price increase is just another scheme in her history of backroom dealings. The public must keep the pressure to make this pip squeak. People want an example of crony capitalism – This is it!

August 28, 2016

The Mind of the Market [Book Review]

As I was finishing *The Mind of the Market* by Michael Shermer (of which I have a signed copy), I was having a discussion with a fellow business major. This hard-headed, toddler-like buffoon was no stranger to less than critical thinking – but since he asked about the book I was reading, I told him. It covers how humans have developed our business morals and markets from our evolutionary past. Then he surprised me with the most arrogant thing he has ever said, "Our world today has no bearing on our past". Don't be like this presumptuous fool! Let me rely on Mr. Shermer to prove otherwise.

The Mind of the Market uses plenty of enjoyable tales, studious studies, and interesting historical facts to show how we have developed our market since the infancy of our species. The tribal instinct used thousands of years ago have stayed with us and even guided how we created our market. Think of it like the "invisible hand" that Adam Smith suggested in The Wealth of Nations.

If you know Michael Shermer, you know he writes in an entertaining way that keeps you reading as well as learning. He is the founder of the Skeptic Society so there are numerous studies to clearly define where he is getting his information. But, since there are so many studies within the book (which I strongly recommend you getting) I will instead focus on his main points in the book.

There are many aspects of numbers and probability that we still have trouble understanding – all from our primitive upbringing. In Accounting, there is a term called "sunk costs" which are expenses put into a project or asset that cannot be returned. When approached with the problem of whether or not the project or asset should be kept even though it is unlikely to be successful, people are far more likely to stick with the project. It is like gambling. When facing losses, one is more likely to stay with it to try to recoup losses. But this is completely illogical and hard to get away from. I was even taught this in college.

We also base decisions about a whole population on small numbers of data. These mistakes are apparent in daily stock traders and even politicians. The example Shermer used was picking red and white marbles out of two bags. If the bags were split 1/3 and 1/3 of each color in each bag – pulling out 5 marbles would usually satisfy our curiosity. We would draw the conclusion of the marbles in each bag based on our findings. This again, is not always correct.

There is also the "framing effect" where we base decisions on how the offer is framed. Here is the example from the book:

    1. Phones-are-Us offers the new DgiMusicCam cell phone for $100; five blocks away FactoryPhones has the same model half off for $50. Do you make the trip to save $50?

    2. Laptops-are-Us offers the new carbon fiber computer for $1000; five blocks away CompuBlessings has the same model discounted to $950. Do you make the trip to save $50?

Most would make the trip for the first one, but very few would make the trip for the other one even though you are saving $50 each time. Shermer calls this "mental accounting" where we compute the reward versus the effort. This framing is used everywhere but especially in commercials or in sales pitches.

Other tribal-like characteristics like this include:

Best sellers – We trust best seller lists because others have deemed the product good so we value that. Just like if a tribe of humans are all eating something, we conclude that the food is good.

Trusting celebrities – Just like we used to trust tribal leaders, we trust celebrities today to show us quality products and because they use it too, we find the product worthy.

Trusting people like us – Because it was wise to only trust your kin and tribe, we have a deep sense of trust for people like ourselves. Some scientists think this may be where our racist tendencies comes from. Luckily, we are now smart enough to resist racism (well, the more intelligent of our species).

Moral fairness – We come from a long history of banding together and sharing our hard work. Even today, we desperately want people to work and put something into the system. We hate freeloaders! Similarly, we desire those who are more wealthy to share more with us – even though they earned it.

I think the most profound point in The Mind of the Market is the necessity of the freedom of trade. The freer the market, the freer the people. In every culture, the liberation of the markets have freed the people and even saved nations. The comparison is made, that just like evolution is bottom up design, the market is bottom up and determined by the people. In totalitarian societies, so much effort is to determining the market value of products. Free societies have no such problem. And unlike its totalitarian partner, free capitalist societies are controlled and upheld by the people. In doing this, the markets are free to grow and because it is built into its structure, the free market has incentives to grow.

Shermer uses a quote from one of my favorite Founding Fathers Thomas Jefferson to stress this point, "Freedom is the right to choose, the right to create for oneself the alternative choice. Without the possibility of choice, and the exercise of creation, a man is not a man, but a member, an instrument, a thing."

And finally, the most important aspect of free trade – the global market. As mentioned above, we have a deep sense of tribe-like loyalty. We want to take care of ourselves, our families, our countrymen first. Because it is a deep instinct of ours, it is understandable and in the worst financial downturns, countries always pull back. We turn away from the global market. This is not wise. Take for instance, the creation of the European Union (I may have lost my conservative reader here). Post World War II, the United States and the Soviet Union ruled all. It wasn't until the 1980's and 90's did the

European countries begin to shine because they banded together. By combining their economies, the whole continent prospered to above even the United States. The people prospered and the region prospered. They are now one of the biggest economies – even with such a small area and few resources (compared to the US).

If there is one lesson from this book, it is that we are a product of evolution – and our market is a product of evolution. There must be freedom to choose, "we must choose freedom, then create the circumstances in which it can be realized, and then defend it."

August 28, 2016

Condom Ban Hoax

A story broke that Mike Pence, Vice presidential candidate, wanted to ban condoms. It spread like wild-fire. The quote used was, "If you want to risk ruining your life before it's started, go ahead, gamble with condoms. But I say we need to ban them and make the right decision for those who clearly aren't capable of making it themselves". This quote is not true – a shameless quote out of context. The source (Newslo, Politicalo, and Religionlo) were bad sites and have done this for clicks. The investigative work was done by Kim LaCapria at snopes.com. Despite what you think about the candidates, a skeptical reader should be at least slightly pleased that the truth is shown. And one may feel a slight relief that Mr. Pence (I call him Pence the Credulous) does not actually think we should ban condoms.

If one digs, a controversial quote from 2002 does point to the idea, but in fairness the Mr. Credulous, he does not really suggest we need to ban condoms – he simply wants to promote abstinence in a not-so-subtle Christian plug:

"I mean, at the end of the day, what condoms actually do is they give our kids a false sense of security, they're actually tricking them into thinking they're having safe sex, when in fact, very often, those intercourses result in unwanted teen pregnancies. And the reason why that's happening is because condoms are designed to be hip, to be modern, to be practical and what not, and the truth is that that's a lie. The only way to stay safe from premature pregnancy and sexually-transmitted diseases is to practice abstinence and pray to God, that's the only real way to stay safe," Pence argued. "At the end of the day, it's the unjustified trust in condoms that plays a huge part in abortion rates going through the roof..."

And here is where the misquote comes in:

"If you want to risk ruining your life before it's even started, go ahead, gamble with condoms. But I say we need to ban them and make the right decision for those who clearly aren't capable of making it themselves. What we don't need are condoms that are unsafe; what we DO need are smarter kids"

This quote seems to have been buried in time – only to be brought back to life by shameless lies brought to you by Newslo. Now, with that cleared, we must not forget who really desired the condom banned: The Catholic Church. As if it is a bundled package, the Catholic Church provides healthcare along with its charity. Unfortunately, that means no condoms. Any working brain can imagine what has happened when people are denied condoms as well as AIDS education: people die. Millions die. The working of the Catholic Church has brought suffering to those in Calcutta and greater India, in Kenya, in Rwanda, and missions around the world.

As Christopher Hitchens said in a debate against Archbishop John Onaiyekan, the Roman Catholic Archbishop of Abuja, Nigeria, and the Rt Hon Ann Widdecombe:

"I say it, I say it in the presence of his grace, and I say it to his face the preaching's of his church are responsible for the death and suffering and misery of millions of his brother and sister Africans, and he should apologize for it"

With that said, be on the lookout for these irrational beings that have deemed the condom banned. If they be in a position of power – defy them! No doubt, brain rot like condom bans are just the tip of the gullible irrational iceberg.

August 30, 2016

September 2016

The Kurds: Homeless even at Home

If you already don't like Turkey's current administration, this defiantly won't help. Although they initially refused to assist in the Syrian war or with the ISIS menace, they now wish to intervene – now that the hard fighting is over. And to add even more to it, they are once again assaulting the Kurdish people.

From the very beginning, the Kurds in southeast Turkey and northern Iraq, have been defending land that is not even theirs from ISIS. Although they are the largest minority group without a homeland, the Kurds (men and women) have taken up arms against the radical Islamic group. This is an even bigger feat considering their past.

Remember the Baath party in Iraq and their cruelty towards the Kurds and the Kuwaiti people. It was Saddam Hussein's ethnic cleansing attacks that made the U.S. believe they possessed weapons of mass destruction. Recovering from that, the Kurds also had to deal with oppressive attacks from both Turkey and Iran. The attacks from Turkey were so bad, it was used as one of the reasons the United Nations refused to let Turkey into the UN.

Now, the brave Kurdish people, fighting for land that is not their own, have run into more trouble with Turkey. When Turkey first began interventions in Syria, even Russia showed concerned calling on turkey to avoid strikes in Syria on Syrian Kurds. Minister Omer Celik responded,

"Turkey is a sovereign state, it is a legitimate state. To suggest it is on par with a terrorist organization and suggest there are talks between them, that a deal has been reached between them, this is unacceptable."

Despite its hard fight from Mosul all the way to North Syria, the Kurdish Militia have been ordered – and dare I say *threatened?* – to move out of the area and allow Turkish troops to take charge. The reason being is that the victories seen by the Kurdish forces may be used as patriotic fuel for separatism at home. Despite the assistance the Kurds have received from the U.S. since even the 80's, the Turkish defend their bullying by claiming the U.S. was very supportive in Turkey's general counter ISIS and efforts to secure their borders. The Kurdish, people forever without a home or a voice, must be kept quiet for now. Yet another aggression towards the hard fighting U.S. ally

September 1, 2016

Rigged Election: Can it be True?

Hearing claims that the United States election system is "rigged" is nothing new to 2016 and – seeing that the claims always come from loons – I always disregarded it. But, as the election continues on… I am slowly thinking otherwise. Could the election be rigged? Of course not. But it is absolutely unfair and undemocratic.

Claiming that the election is rigged is such an outlandish statement only because "rigged" infers that there is a plan – an agenda – behind the election. People who claim the election is rigged (the far right and far left) seem to think that there is an invisible hand deciding the fate of each election. Those same people who kicked and screamed that Obama was an outsider are the same people who now think Obama is the system. No matter what happens, conspirators claim the system is rigged. This is how you play tennis without the net.

The very first hint of an unfair election was the Hillary – Sanders conflict. Not to mention the way Bernie and his delegates were treated during the primaries, and the Superdelegate system; Wikileaks has provided us with absolute proof the Democratic Party was actively plotting against Bernie Sanders. Within the Democratic Party emails, there were remarks such as:

"If she outperforms this polling, the Bernie camp will go nuts and allege misconduct. They'll probably complain regardless, actually" regarding New Hampshire primaries

"Wondering if there's a good Bernie narrative for a story, which is that Bernie never ever had his act together, that his campaign was a mess," said DNC official Mark Paustenbach

"This could make several points difference with my peeps. My Southern Baptist peeps would draw a big difference between a Jew and an atheist" said DNC CFO Brad Marshall.

Yes, they were actively planning to use Sander's religion against him. We can no longer assume the Democratic Party is actually Democratic. No rational human being can ever say this process is Democratic. In addition to the primary scam, the issue of Debbie Shultz comes into play. She defiantly had a hand in the Wikileak scandal, but now there is talk as to her connection with Hillary's pick for VP. Hillary was able to get Debbie Shultz in position of party chairman – in return, she was able to influence the primary to get Clinton the nomination. To get Shultz that position, she had to get someone to step down – that was Tim Kaine. Now that Shultz took the hit, Tim Kaine is the Vice Presidential nominee. That is the theory anyway – and it is far more believable now that we know the Democratic Party has a flawed system.

The actions by the Democratic Party is extreme contemptible, immoral, and completely unfair to the candidates and the voters. The party has an agenda to be precisely *un-*

democratic and they should be ashamed. There should be action against them to protect the will of the people. The party seems to have gotten away without any trouble.

Now, with the pitiful excuse for a primary is over, the humble voter has to wonder: how can we be sure the election itself isn't rigged. There seems to be no way to know that third parties are being treated fairly. Despite one's political views, fair elections are absolutely necessary for a democratic country. Without one – we are in a banana republic – unsure that our votes mean anything.

I am not saying that we should be jumping to the extreme conclusion that the whole system is worthless, just that we must take all conspiracies and information with a grain of salt – or rather a cellar of salt.

September 2, 2016

Mother Teresa – Saint of Suffering

No doubt there is a lot of talk about Mother Teresa of Calcutta. She is a symbol of charity and care – and yet she is the exact opposite. Lurking in the shadows of the news, there are tons of articles about how Mother Teresa really is – but I want to include my list of misdeeds from Saint Teresa.

1) "Suffering is a gift from God"

Mother Teresa honestly believed suffering is a gift from God, there for, assisting any pain of death or sickness is taking away that gift. She once said to a dying patient, "Pain and suffering have come into your life, but remember pain, sorrow, suffering are but the kiss of Jesus – a sign that you have come so close to Him that He can kiss you" to which the patient replied, "can you tell your Jesus to stop kissing me?" One must not forget that when this Saint passed, it was not in her "house of the dying" – it was in one of the world's best facilities.

One instance of blatant disregard for her patients, when a building was donated, fully furnished with the best beds and equipment, Teresa and staff threw out all furnishings and replaced them with sleeping bags and cots. Everything from medicine for AIDs patients to simple furnishings, Mother Teresa loved suffering.

"There is something beautiful in seeing the poor accept their lot, to suffer it like Christ's Passion. The world gains much from their suffering" – Mother Teresa

2) Mother Teresa was a fraudster

Her organizations received about $100 million in annual receipts – and yet her patients lacked any pain medication, any medical education (definitely not condoms or sexual education), or any comforting bedding in which to die. In fact, the rooms for her dying children were windowless, bed less cold rooms. It was in this room where her "miracle" was "witnessed". The room was dark and packed with sick people and a single hanging light bulb – when a picture was taken, the light produced a halo above her... yup, and that was her "miracle".

The Missionaries of Charity always relied on charities. Food, clothes, etc were all provided by donations. So this $100 million seems to have been kept by the Vatican Bank – never to see the light of day (kind of like the dying at Calcutta).

3) Mother Teresa: the friend of dictators

No one can forget the relationship the Catholic Church had with the Axis powers – but their love for abusive dictators still hasn't ended. Especially with Mother Teresa.
When Indian Prime Minister Indira Gandhi's suspended civil liberties in 1975, Mother Teresa said, "People are happier. There are more jobs. There are no strikes." Mother Teresa's comments were even criticized outside India within the Catholic media Indira Gandhi's.

Teresa flew all the way to Haiti to visit Dictator Jean-Claude Duvalier who donated tons of the people's money to her cause. As if he people of Haiti weren't suppressed enough. Teresa also took money from Robert Maxwell, a corrupt publisher who was later convicted for embezzling $450 million. When asked for the money back so the money could be returned to the victim's, Mother Teresa refused to return it.

4) Mother Teresa had no respect for the dying

Along with denying the sick when medication, comfort, and care – Mother Teresa was also involved with secret baptisms. Her and her staff would baptize the dying in their sleep or before death. A member of her staff reported, "Sisters were to ask each person in danger of death if he wanted a 'ticket to heaven'. An affirmative reply was to mean consent to baptism. The sister was then to pretend that she was just cooling the patient's head with a wet cloth, while in fact she was baptizing him, saying quietly the necessary words. Secrecy was important so that it would not come to be known that Mother Teresa's sisters were baptizing Hindus and Muslims."

The people of India also saw Mother Teresa as a symbol of lingering colonization because she supported the suspension of civil liberties among other things. Historian Vijay Prashad wrote, "When it comes to saving the poor, the dark bodies are again invisible, for the media seem to celebrate only the worn out platitudes of such as Mother Teresa and ignore the struggles of those bodies for their own liberation. To open the life of someone like Mother Teresa to scrutiny, therefore, is always difficult. [...] Mother Teresa's work was part of a global enterprise for the alleviation of bourgeois guilt, rather than a genuine challenge to those forces that produce and maintain poverty."

Of all the Popes to make Mother Teresa a saint, it is surprising that it is the most humanist Pope Francis. But do not forget the corrupt, immoral, disregard for human life. Christopher Hitchens was correct when he said, "Mother Teresa wasn't a friend of the poor, she is a friend of poverty".

September 4, 2016

Overworked Americans

I haven't been able to write a post in a few days because I am working a job I hate until I can start a job I love – so I decided to write a post about working. It turns out that Americans work more than any other industrialized country.

There was an interesting piece written by economist John Maynard Keynes in called, "Economic Possibilities for our Grandchildren" in which he predicted that the economy would become so productive that we would barely need to work at all. Based on his theory, as technology keeps improving – people will need to work less and less. This shift is mainly due to automation or to cheap labor. The shift has already happened – in fact, since Keynes wrote the essay the average workweek went from around 50 hours a week in 1930 to 40 in 1970. And there it has stayed. Juliet Schor actually calculated that Americans work about a month more per year than in 1970. So why hasn't the trend continued till today?

Everyone disregards such studies claiming that workers are simply whining – but when Americans work more that the English, the French, and extremely more than the Germans, Norwegians and even the Japanese – These studies beg more attention. The Bureau of Labor Statistics reported that more than 25 million Americans — 20.5 percent of the total workforce — reported they worked at least 49 hours a week in 1999. Eleven millions of those said they worked more than 59 hours a week. And yet, only 26% of Americans feel they are over-worked. Experts say this is simply an illusion.

So why hasn't America moved to a more leisurely life style? Benjamin Freedman, a Harvard economist said, "the U.S. economy is right on track to reach Keynes's eight-fold multiple" by the year 2029. He set out to figure out why the increased production we have been seeing has not yet translated into more leisure time. He remarks that the claim Americans just want more money to buy the next best thing is, "at best, far from sufficient."

Friedman finally determined that the standard of living would continue to rise for everyone but the prediction he made that Keynes's "eight-fold" figure would hold up – but not for the median American worker. He predicted that by 2029, it is likely to by only 3.5 of that Keyes predicted. That is because the gains in productivity are not equally distributed among all workers. Those at the top benefit the most, whereas those who perform for manual work are stuck working longer hours. So next time you miss my wonderful posts, you will know why.

September 9, 2016

The Price for Civilization

The controversial topic of the death penalty in the United States has been growing strong over the years, and yet the penalty still remains solid with in the court system and in practice, particularly in Texas. This final and absolute solution to heinous crimes remains a problem because of the very real threat of false convictions. With the use of DNA evidence and even added or non-factual eyewitness reports, numerous convicted individuals are being exonerated from their fate. These individuals, facing the death penalty for crimes they did not commit dodged a huge bullet, no pun intended. But even with these very real sob stories, can the death penalty still be used in our justice system? To answer that question, one cannot rely completely on pathos-induced thought process.

Hopefully not out of arrogance, my view on capital punishment has always been a favorable one. This may be due to my upbringing in the Southern United States and without much exposure to impoverished social economic areas to which the death penalty seems to be the most prevalent (1). But because I feel so strongly for it, I must keep insisting until proven otherwise that the death penalty is an acceptable form of punishment for the most heinous of criminals. Of course there must be a limit to whom and what is deemed punishable by death. An opponent to my position may quickly think "what if the criminal does not deserve it" or "does the death penalty deter crime" and other questions along that line such as the arguments proposed in innocanceproject.org. Any arguments for or against the death penalty should really be focused on the philosophical aspect of the death penalty and not on the clear misuse of it. I will, however, discuss the threat of incorrect rulings, as they must be taken into consideration. I will also cover whether it deters crime and common arguments against the death penalty as well as discuss some convicted innocence cases and answer the big question: should capital punishment continue to be imposed when though there is a chance that an innocent person could be put to death for a crime they did not commit?

To set the tone of my argument for the death penalty, I must add that this is a very serious topic and anyone erroneously for or against capital punishment cannot be taken seriously. J.R.R. Tolkien, in Lord of the Rings, beautifully words it, "Many that live deserve death. And some that die deserve life. Can you give it to them? Then do not be too eager to deal out death in judgment" (2), which is to say, that there will be people that live and deserve death and others who are purely innocent that are unfairly put to death. Innoccanceproject.org provides 333 cases in which have since been repealed due to a number of reasons, but the number one reason is Eyewitness Misidentification (3).

The best story about this life threatening mistake is the misidentification of Marvin Anderson. This horrendous case took place in 1982 before DNA evidence was widely used or reliable. Marvin Anderson was questioned about a rape that occurred in the past week. He was mistakenly convicted because of the racial assumptions of police and the mistaken identification from the victim. As a result, Marvin was convicted of two counts of rape, forcible sodomy, abduction, and robbery for which he was completely innocent (4). This outrageous claim by the victim very well could have ended an innocent man's life. The justice system's spectacular and unreasonable ruling based on this woman's unclear accusation is absolutely unacceptable and gives the anti-death penalty party every reason to object to the idea of using capital punishment. But it must be suggested that using these situations from Innocence Project for fantastic misuse of the justice system and its capital punishment option is an inadequate argument for the abolishment of the death penalty. Relying on such extreme cases may very well be the reason why the death penalty is still around after so many objections over the years.

An echoing argument for and against the death penalty is the topic of deterrence. Whether the death penalty actually does deter crime can be a smoking gun for either party. An interesting case of widely used successful capital punishment would be from the Indian Rebellion of 1857. At this point, European and more specifically English rule had reached a breaking point for colonial India. Several groups of opposition such as Hindu and Muslim sepoys, took arms against the Crown and set up initiation policies in which a British Officer, Soldier, or citizens must be killed to join (Raghavan, 2005). To combat this effective and deadly force, the British used what is commonly known as "blowing from a gun". Originally a Mongrel form of capital punishment, the victim is tied to the muzzle of a cannon with their back pressed against the opening. The British imposed this order, "to fire off at the mouth of cannon the leader of the thieves who was made prisoner, that others may be deterred" (5). Although many British officers saw this barbaric and serious form of punishment as going too far, the results were successful pacifying of revolts (6) and did not struggle with serious opposition even up until Indian Independence in 1947.

Now, this one serious and over exaggerated example of deterrence is only used to show the wide reaching possibilities of the death penalty, and I am in no way suggesting this as an actual solution to crime. Mentioned in the beginning of this essay, anyone can easily be mistaken as a criminal. To suggest deterrence occurred within the United States, one does not have to look as far back. The United States Supreme Court outlawed the use of capital punishment from 1972 with the notable case of Furman v. Georgia until 1976, when the lights went out in Georgia, and capital punishment was reinstated with the landmark case of Gregg v. Georgia (7). The crimes per capita and executions show a direct correlation throughout those times (8) and although this may be only one case in which an anti-capital punishment individual may dismiss as irrelevant, the figures cannot be ignored.

Another point I would like to make is: how many murders must be deterred to successfully win support for capital punishment? Surely killing just one murderer would appeal to the average person as a sufficient means by which to put the victim and their families at ease. The difficult figure to prove is how many crimes are really deterred? I could give examples such as Arthur Shawcross who, after paroled from his 15 year sentence for the rape of two children, took 11 more lives before being arrested again, but any case like this will be subjected to dismissal among those against the death penalty (9). And it is true: no one can ever accurately find that number of lives saved by the death penalty, but I plead with the reader to assume the death of the criminal is justified in that the victims and communities are put at ease and the actions of the criminal can never be repeated.

The final argument in opposition to the death penalty that must be covered is whether or not the criminal acted in a rational and logical manner when committing the crime which echoes the argument against punishing mentally ill criminals. Knee-jerk reply would be to say, they committed the crime, they have to face the consequences. But let me reference another story. Jennifer Ertman and Elizabeth Pena, 14 and 16 were coming home from school in Houston, Texas when they took a shortcut and were attacked by six men including Peter Cantu and 14 year-old Raul Villarreal. The next hour was hell for these two teenage girls who were repeatedly raped in such a way there was "never less than 2 men on one girl". Peter Cantu strung up the girls with belts and shoelaces and forced the 14 year old Raul Villarreal to join in as part of initiation to their gang. Finally, after attempting to kill the girls where complaints such as "the bitch won't die" were noted, the two girls died together. To end the details and save the reader the gruesome scene, it should be noted that the gang members were boasting about the "virgin blood on them". The five men were convicted and sentenced to death in Harris County (the Juvenile's case will be reviewed when he turns 18) (10). There are numerous stories such as these. The convicted individual gets free representation whereas the victim lies dead and the opposition to capital punishment dares to claim the convicted criminal was not thinking rationally and such a capital punishment decision is unfair or too harsh. How dare anyone say that death is undeserving of crimes like these? The audacity of anyone who says criminals aren't thinking rationally. After free, seemingly unlimited, State-provided representation, criminals are convicted and people have the nerve to say they don't deserve punishment if it includes their death because they weren't thinking rationally. That, as victims such as Jennifer Ertman and Elizabeth Pena beg for their lives, Peter Cantu and his gang should be taken lightly because they may not have been thinking rationally. I am sorry, but neither I, nor any other rationally thinking, moral individual can consider treating men and women like these with anything other than the most serious of punishment.

It is completely understandable that someone may not support the death penalty because it is too harsh or unfitting, and of course, absolute. The best and most sensible reason to oppose the death penalty is the chance an innocent defendant may be wrongfully sentenced to death. But with the numerous violent and barbaric crimes, it must remain an option. With the continual advancement in DNA and effective justice systems, wrongful sentencing can and will be avoided. With careful, just, and swift action against the worst offenders, the modern era can implement capital punishment as a useful and effective price for civilization.

September 10, 2016

Thomas Jefferson and the Tripoli Pirates [Book Review]

"This is the story of how a new nation, saddled with war debt and desperate to establish credibility, was challenged by four Muslim powers. Our merchant ships were captured and the crews enslaved. Despite its youth, America would do what established western powers chose not to do: stand up to intimidation and lawlessness."

In America's infancy, there were huge difficulties establishing itself on the global stage; but none more challenging and defining than the war with the Tripoli pirates. Along with providing the reader personal details into Thomas Jefferson's life, authors Brian Kilmeade and Don Yaeger, also laid out the first foreign conflict in American history – which has determined our political future since.

The war of the Barbary Coast Pirates included four powers: Morocco, Algeria, Tripoli, and Tunisia with a central focus around the Ottomans in Istanbul. The four powers, using the authority of the Quran, attacked and raided merchant ships and enslaved the crew. The part of the Quran used to justify this barbarism reads, "all nations which had not acknowledged the Prophet were sinners, whom it was the right and duty of the faithful to plunder and enslave." Any nation who does not pay uncertain tributes to the pirates are at risk of losing trade and citizens. The tribute paid was never a set amount and was always subject to increasing at any time – and further more – a tribute to one of the four countries does not guarantee safety with the other countries. The slow communication also proved to complicate things.

Over 1.25 million slaves were taken hostage between the 16th and 18th centuries – and since the Treaty of Paris, which ended the war of independence with Great Britain, American trade was protected by the French. But, come 1800, the aspiring American merchant ships became targets. Once taken, the Barbary Pirates would sell all cargo and parade their victims throughout the streets – their futures unknown. Having a deep sympathy for freedom, Thomas Jefferson – then the ambassador to France – attempted to make peace with the four states. After a few years, the negotiations were ready to begin. Envoys were sent to pay for the release of the American hostages – only to be let down. The Barbary States demanded $660,000 each for free travel through the Mediterranean. Unfortunately, the struggling indebted nation only allocated about $40,000 for negotiations.

Jefferson, seeing that negotiations were less than fruitful, convinced Washington and the first Congress to begin building a navy. In the meanwhile, Congressional coffers finally got the hostages released for about $1 million – after a decade of captivity. In negotiations, Americans were reminded who they were dealing with: Tripolitan ambassador Sidi Haji Abdrahaman explains,

"It was written in their Koran, that all nations which had not acknowledged the Prophet were sinners, whom it was the right and duty of the faithful to plunder and enslave; and that every mussulman who was slain in this warfare was sure to go to paradise. He said, also, that the man who was the first to board a vessel had one slave over and above his share, and that when they sprang to the deck of an enemy's ship,

every sailor held a dagger in each hand and a third in his mouth; which usually struck such terror into the foe that they cried out for quarter at once."

In response, Jefferson wrote an all too accurate portrayal of America's newest enemies, *"Money is their god, and Muhammad their prophet"* – he understood their motives and was ready for war. When Jefferson became the third president of the United States, the navy was ready for war. His insights into the religious extremist mindset helped prepare Jefferson, and the nation, for war to settle this dispute once and for all. The United States was determined to defeat these pirates in a way none of the Europeans could. In an unusual prediction in regards to confronting Islam, Jefferson noted, *"We* ought not to *fight them at* all unless *we* determine to *fight them forever"*

The incredible story of American ingenuity and bravery in the face of a stronger and richer enemy, Kilmeade and Yaeger create an easy and enjoyable read. If all history books were written like this, history classes would be far more popular. A final and lesser known fact covered in this forgotten war was the deeply held secular beliefs held by Jefferson and the first Congress. The Treaty of Tripoli was written and ratified by congress that, "The government of the United States of America is not in any sense founded on the Christian religion"

This and many more little known facts of America's foundation are hidden throughout history – and Thomas Jefferson and the Tripoli Pirates is an incredibly orchestrated book that sheds light on this little known part of America's past. There needs to be more books like this one. This book is recommended to all history lovers as well as those who wish to love history. For one cannot understand the present, without first understanding the past.

September 13, 2016

NDPL Misinformation

Everyone has heard about the Native American protest in North Dakota – and the cause is very legitimate – but the people I speak to and see online seem to be under a misconception regarding the whole event.

First off, the confrontation is right outside of the Standing Rock reservation for the Sioux Indians. The Dakota Access Pipeline is a 1,172 mile pipeline that has the potential to transport over 500,000 barrels of oil a day – saving uncountable amounts of money on 18-wheeler transportation (not to mention, the environmental impact these 18-wheelers have). The project was already approved by the government to cross the Missouri River – and here is the best part – the pipeline crosses over a mile north of the reservation.

Source: Energy Transfer Partners   LARIS KARKLIS/THE WASHINGTON POST

Too often do I hear complaints that the government is taking more land away from the reservation – which is completely false. Arguments like this are an easy way to discover someone has no idea what they are talking about. And this protest, taking place on public land, has recently been causing more problems. The first reported act of violence has been reported – the protesters attacked! Four private security guards and police dogs have been injured when over a hundred protesters confronted them.

Again, more reports of protesters being injured are circulating without any proof. The Sioux spokesman, Sitting Bear, has reported that 5 protesters and one child have been bitten by security dogs and that at least 30 protesters have been pepper sprayed by security guards – which is a big deal considering the guards are not policemen. If the protesters were pepper sprayed, there would be grounds for assault charges. And yet, there were no reports of such events. Sitter Bear never reported it!

Could it be that the protesters couldn't prove any violence from the police? Even more, the National Guard has been sent to the area to control the situation in a more professional way. This is a rational reaction from the government because of the many complaints. But the ones who are worried are the protesters! The National Guard would protect them against any brutality and could properly handle confrontations – but the protesters are up in arms! Could it be that they do not want the authorities involved? Of course it is.

This protest has even become a political movement. Amy Goodman, executive producer and host of Democracy Now! Has a warrant for her arrest for trespassing. Jill Stein has a warrant for trespassing, and mischief in connection to the protest in North Dakota.

It should be noted that: yes, the Sioux have the right to protest. They have the right to be worried. But it must be said that the North Dakota Pipeline is NOT of tribal lands; brutality has not been reported; protesters ARE breaking laws; the pipeline has been approved and can save a lot of money. The facts are important!

September 14, 2016

Judge Persky's Failure

Brock Turner is officially an American enemy – streets and online forums alike are on fire with outrage over the Stanford University rape case in which Turner raped a unconscious woman and only getting 6 months in prison. This call to arms has become a wakeup call to feminists, college students, and humanists alike. The rage over the injustice has resulted in non-stop protests outside of Turner's house. An ironic turn of events because the judge didn't want to ruin the young man's life because of this one mistake – and now his life is truly ruined (for now).

It becomes truly hard to imagine a fitting punishment for this pitiful miserable man when our justice system fails us – and especially fails the victim. But the rage really must be aimed appropriately – the incredibly horrendous and unforgivable act Turner committed is done, but the actions by the one who we trusted to punish him is not. Judge Aaron Persky is the one who had power to bring justice to Turner and for his victim. And yet, so much work is being done to protest and humiliate Turner – not that he doesn't deserve it, but more so that Judge Persky deserves it more. Judge Persky had what Turner probably didn't: time to think his actions over in a rational and unbiased setting – and he still fails to carry out justice.

First started by Stanford law professor Michele Dauber, more appropriate and useful actions have been taken against the ridiculous judge. The movement's objective is to recall Persky from office, or at least get the California Commission on Judicial Performance to begin investigations for misconduct. There are even more splinter organizations rallying to hold Persky accountable such as recall aaronpersky.com.

The case must be looked at in its entirety to fully form a conclusion about the judge. In California, the maximum for "sexual penetration and assault with the intent to commit rape" is 14 years in jail whereas to minimum is 2 years and is reserved for unusual circumstances. Due to the seemingly unclear and strange situation in which the crime was committed, the prosecution demanded Turner be jailed for 6 years. Judge Persky ruled that Turner serve 6 months in jail followed by 3 years of probation. Turner is also ordered to register with California as a sexual offender.

The biggest defense Turner gave was that he was under the influence of drugs and alcohol. Apparently, the young swimmer has a record of drug use and under-age drinking in high school as well as a history of making "aggressive and unwanted sexual advances" on women. It was the drug use and the party scene that drove Turner to commit the irreversible and life changing crime of rape – but is the situation an excuse for his crime? Can anyone listen to the victim's testimony and still sympathize with Turner? Apparently Judge Persky can.

When it comes down to it: no, Judge Persky probably didn't commit misconduct while Judge – but, the people he presides over can no longer expect rational rulings from him. His community that elected him cannot know whether justice can be carried out by Persky. Which is why any rage must be aimed toward the Judge. He dropped the ball, he was the only obstacle standing in the way of justice and he unashamed failed. And that point alone is a fearful thought for victims everywhere.

September 19, 2016

Dr. Phillip Stetz – A Review

[NOTE: This is a review I wrote for a Professor I had. Just uploading it here because it was funny - This post turned out to be one of my most popular post for the first half of the year]

Professor Phillip Stetz has been at Stephen F Austin State University ("SFA") since 2002 and has been an associate professor since 2008 and although he has received high praise from few sources (mainly from himself), under further review, anyone can see and surely does see that he is a joke to the department and is anything but helpful to students. In fact, he is the lowest rated professor in the college of business we can see why. His outdated expertise is unhelpful and defiantly unavailable to students. If a student is unlucky enough as to take this professor (usually because all the other professors fill up so quickly to avoid his course) they will have the opportunity to take the worst professor known to SFA, and the college of business is finally catching on.

After calling his own son a 'pussy' for switching jobs, one should first point to his faculty vita: a long list of repetitive, half-truths, that mean to show his professional expertise but merely leave the student to wonder "how is this guy tenured?". His son, having worked four years at a Big Four Accounting Firm outshines his dad who worked only two years at a Big Eight Accounting Firm Coopers and Lybrand. Maybe, in his seniority, he forgot this fact before throwing his son under the bus in front of his class? No, this is merely an introduction to the character of Phillip Stetz. Any former student should add "hypocrite" to his name. I also recall his advice that, in the professional world, you should stay with a firm for no less than 5 years in order to be a faithful employee.

Those who can't do, teach. Nothing rings louder than this saying for professor Stetz who, in 1975 after ending his unsuccessful career in Auditing and Tax, began his reign over the family business: Stetz's Enterprises. Although one may quickly see there was a "660% growth" in the company, Professor Stetz closed the company in 1990. Maybe the growth was too much for humble Stetz? In any case, Dr. Stetz closed the business in a hurry to begin his long bout of unemployment and to go back to school to get his master's and doctorate degrees. Why would Stetz close an apparently successful business venture that has lasted generations just to become unemployed for multiple years? It was not actually successful. If it were successful, he would not close his business. Perhaps it would be good advice to Stetz to have him take his own class. If one took his class MGT 463, he gives a semester's worth of excuses as to why businesses fail. This must be his biggest area of expertise because while he boasts of being an entrepreneurial professional, he definitely knows how to fail in a career and in business.

If his students were each made into a metaphor as an entrepreneurial business run by Dr. Stetz, even he would admit and has admitted to them that they are not prepared for success; and he is proud of it! In my evaluation of Professor Stetz, I quickly covered his competency as a professor:

If I could give one bad evaluation in my entire college career, it would be for professor Stetz. He is unhelpful and proud of it. He provides vague lectures and answers no questions in class. If a brave soul is crazy enough to attempt to talk to professor Stetz outside of class, they will be greeted by the most unpleasant professor at SFA. He will do nothing short of screaming and throwing things to avoid meeting with students during his office hours. The students are all on their own against this vindictive, arrogant, outdated, malevolent, bully of a professor. If these evaluations were taken seriously, he would no longer be teaching at SFA.

And perhaps these evaluations were taken very seriously by the department. According to a few management professors, who informed me anonymously, he is equally as unpleasant to his coworkers as he is to his students. Additionally, his core class, which has been taught by him and only him, is now offered by three other professors and his once open selection of classes is replaced by only one class period. Meaning, the department is catching on and started phasing him out – good for them!

Because very little feedback is available, only ratemyprofessor provides a true look at what the students think of this man. Graded on his helpfulness, clarity, and easiness from a 1 to 5, professor Stetz stands out as the lowest ranking teacher in the department of management, college of business, as well as the SFA Campus as a whole. Out of 31 ratings, he has an average of 2.1. Seems his coworkers and students both see his stain on the department and are reeling him back in from a position of any sort of usefulness. To parallel the very *very* few positive feedback Stetz conveniently provides on his own faculty vita, students here often say:

Absolutely the worst professor I have ever taken. He is extremely unhelpful and is incredibly rude to students. – 11/09/2015

Worst professor I've ever taken! He is a professor who only helps males. Whenever I would go ask questions he would say read the book or ask your classmates (Even if I came in with a question from the book). My guy friends however, would get help. If you didn't pass and you take his class your adviser understands why you didn't pass. – 08/29/2015

He has the experience and expertise but does not share it with his students. He waves it in the student's face and gets a kick out of students that try to grab it. His way of teaching is outdated, dated from 2002 at the latest. If this were the 90's he'd be top notch. Don't bother challenging or sharing new, creative ideas; they will be wrong. – 02/02/2015

Worst experience I have ever had at SFA! The material was very simple, but he tries to make it hard. Tests are almost all T/F. Won't answer questions, won't help you (even if you go by during office hours). The second B in my college career despite an understanding of the subject. – 04/27/2009

by the far the worst professor I have had in my 4 years at SFA. DO NOT TAKE. Entertains questions but will roll his eyes, tell you to recall a lecture from months prior

*and then never answers it. kept me from ever asking a question even in the confidence
of an e mail or in his office. -05/13/2009*

I can almost hear his airy, nasal, sadistic laugh when reading these. Taking pride in his
failures is only the beginning of why professor Stetz should not be at SFA and his record
proves it. In a clear recollection of the business simulation I participated in his class,
over 1,700 teams were compared nationally online. Over a decade of teams (about five
every class giving him over 50 teams) to compete nationally, he has never had a
successful team. In a rage of frustration for the reality of this lack of teaching
competency, he chewed us out for not performing better for the class period (nothing
new if the reader has had a childish professor). In an anxious and helpless plea of help
in a different class, Professor Stetz refused to help multiple teams in their struggle. So,
in addition to his bullying during class and abuse for seeking help, the Professor will
happily fail you. And if you are to perform poorly in his class, a failing grade as well as a
point reduction in the project grade is all too easy for him to hand out. I say again, "The
students are all on their own against this vindictive, arrogant, outdated, malevolent,
bully of a professor"

This explicitly horrible professor, having received tenure after doing time at SFA, is put
into a position of professional responsibility. The position of tenure is a professional
contract between Stetz and the College of Business where the department gives Stetz a
guarantee of employment in exchange for his continued work as a professor and
continued academic work. Can Dr. Stetz who, with disregard to his lectures, continually
fails to provide his students the best possible service, still hold up his end of the tenure-
bargain? Most professors at SFA do, Dr. Stetz does not. Again, we must look to his
faculty vita.

Just as repetitive and vague as his doctoral dissertation (being titled *An Examination of
Strategies Across the Spectrum of Diversified Corporation,*one can get an idea how
boring and unnecessarily complex his lectures are), his faculty vita is rattled with
journal writings he has published. His profile provides a little over eight original articles
and writings he has contributed. I say *original* articles because he actually, by mistake
or by vanity, repeated many of his articles throughout his profile. Most contributions
consist of fewer than ten pages and co-authored leaves the reader wondering how much
work he actually produced. Are his classes so hard as to steal his effort away from these
academic works? No, of course not. His power points, facts, and lectures look as old as
him and date no later than 2005; far from accurate. If I may repeat the evaluation for
emphasis: "His way of teaching is outdated, dated from 2002 at the latest. If this were
the 90's he'd be top notch. Don't bother challenging or sharing new, creative ideas; they
will be wrong"

Dr. Stetz's favorite work is A-*1 Lanes and Currency Crisis of the East Asian
Tigers* published in 2008 in the Entrepreneurship Theory and Practice Journal
weighing in at 12 pages. Unlike his doctoral dissertation, Dr. Stetz has had help in this
work and so it is not as repetitive nor a massive waste of time to read. The article is
mentioned no less than six times in the vita and yet has failed to put any impression or
emphasis in the work toward the university that so kindly tenured the professor in trust
he will provide some sort of return. According to *Washington times* columnist David

Levy in his 2012 article, *Do College Professors Work Hard Enough*, Professor Stetz has also failed in his academic work. Having 22 weeks of time to work on articles in one year, Dr. Stetz only provided seven articles (totaling 69 pages) over six years. What is he doing other than milking his tenure?

Let us not neglect the rest of his profile or we may miss some sort of meaning to Dr. Stetz's career. Passing his attempt to seem valuable in his long list of "professional services", we find his services to SFA. Fortunately, professor Stetz stopped his repetitive rambling and has gotten to the meat of his service to SFA. Listing "Course Coordinator", "Advisor", and "Mentor" is a stretch made by our professor to seem useful by fulfilling his basic functions as professor. Sparing Stetz the criticism of his own lecturing, we should focus on his role as an advisor and mentor. Please rely on the, again anonymous, feedback from his students. One of whom actually approached Stetz's office during office hours and was yelled at for merely asking to advise on major projects. As a mentor, Stetz attributes his skill in resume preparation, interview techniques, and phone interviews as being a valuable mentor to his students.

His last failure I wish to cover is regarding his attempt to open an Entrepreneurial center at the College of Business. As phrased in the vita:

Although the initial funding was withdrawn for the proposed Entrepreneurial Center, several candidates have been identified who may be interested in changing their career paths to become the new director of the center, once funding is identified

Finally our professor has been brief but honest in his failures. No examples say to why it failed is stated but it can easily be imagined by the reader if one refers to his teaching philosophy. This toad of a professor, if he can be caught in his office during his office hours, will turn away any student who begs for help. The multiple and consistent occurrences of his brutal "help" he provides students proves he not only is a failure as a course coordinator, advisor, mentor, provider of special (or ordinary) accommodation requests, and as a decent human being. Dr. Stetz has failed on all accounts: as a professor, as an advisor, as a mentor, as a tenured employee at SFA, as a business owner, and as an employee.

Again, I must say and the reader must be wondering why Stetz is still at SFA. If the evaluations are taken seriously, the campus will be enlightened to rid of Dr. Stetz. The fast growing and innovative campus has been gifted with new programs and magnificent buildings. The hard working and effortless work of most tenured professors at SFA can be compared only to these successes. Whereas Dr. Stetz's contributions can only be compared to the stale urine stained floors in the library bathrooms, all students are more than aware of.

September 20, 2016

Let's Talk Tax: Clinton vs Trump's Plans

Let's talk about everyone's favorite topic: Taxation! With the 2016 election coming fast, let me explain what Clinton and Trump's tax plans are and what it means for you.

As you can imagine, the two presidential plans are complete opposites - staying loyal to party lines. Trump's plan focuses on tax cuts in the form of lowering tax rates whereas Clinton takes her plan right out of Bernie Sander's book by vowing to raise taxes substantially on the super wealthy.

Trump's Plan

"I am proposing an across-the-board income tax reduction especially for middle-income Americans. This will lead to millions of new and really good-paying jobs. The rich will pay their fair share, but no one will pay so much that it destroys jobs or undermines our ability as a nation to compete."

Donald Trump plans to create only three tax brackets to appeal to the middle class. The Top rate will be 33% (down from 39.6%); the next rate will be 25%; the last will be 12% (most Americans) and anyone earning under $29,000 will pay 0% tax rate. That's right, the bottom earners will pay nothing! A surprising fact to most Trump haters. In fact, NPR recently posted a bias page saying, "much of the savings going to the wealthiest households". Both candidates are jokes, don't get me wrong - but it has turned into a game of "what can we get away with?"

Clinton's Plan

Because she can't steal anymore ideas from Bernie, Clinton has not yet expressed how she will help the middle class. But the jist of her plan is to tax the super wealthy as a way to fund subsidized college tuition and other programs. A good idea, but we defiantly need more details - but details are not her strong suit.

Clinton hopes to implement what Obama could not (she is taking other's ideas again): the Buffet rule which would create a new tax bracket of 43.6% for taxpayers making over $5 million. The next would be 39.6%; 35%l and 33%. The middle class rates would be 28% for earnings over $91,150, 25% for earnings over $37,650, and 15% for earnings over $9275. Clinton also plans for a 0% rate for taxpayers earning $9,275. Another part of her plan I remember quite distinctly is an Exit Tax which aims to punish corporations that leave the U.S. This would be her way of justifying her high tax rates.

What does it all mean?

The big picture for Trumps plan is lower taxes for everyone. It focuses on promoting a healthier business environment to encourage hiring. Clinton's plan is increasing taxes progressively to increase revenue and fund programs. The two plans are as difficult to compare as the candidates themselves - it is Trickle-down economics vs government programs.

The good part about Clinton's plan is that it would add about $1.1 trillion in revenue over 10 years. The bad is that we still don't know her whole plan and I find it difficult to trust that the added revenue would actually make it to the deficit. The good part about Trump's plan is that taxes are cut across the board putting money in the pockets of Americans. But it would reduce the amount of taxes collected by $4.4 Trillion. But it is important to remember that taxes are not the only way to lower the deficit - Trump plans to cut spending and negotiate trade deals (which is as unclear as Clinton's government programs).

In both cases, there is still some uncertainty; but to sum it up: Trump will lower taxes - Clinton will raise them. It seems that Clinton's plan will not affect the average American's tax return directly - but we risk her spending to negate the revenue she will generate. In the end, it seems that Trump's plan will most benefit the average American if he can cut spending. But stay tuned the the debate coming up on the 26th to see what they really have in store.

September 21, 2016

You Get What You Vote For

One can't ignore it. The painful cringe on everyone's faces as they grudgingly support with Donald Trump or Hillary Clinton. On one hand, we have a flamboyant tough guy who's ego wouldn't fit in an Olympic stadium - and on the other hand, we have a corrupt crippled robot who would, and has, said anything to get into office. The two party system has been rotting away and has finally failed completely giving us a buffoon and a robot. But these deplorable candidates have not earned our vote - they are not entitled to our vote. Decades of voting for the "lesser-of-two-evils" has produced failures as candidates and failures as presidents. It is time for something different.

Donald Trump

What can be said about Donald Trump? He has gotten away with uncountable amounts of ridiculous brain rot - he has convinced normal rational people that he is the only answer. If anyone else spouted the amount of garbage he has, they would lose their minds! Trump's character alone has produced unimaginable amounts of craziness - including insulting captured soldiers, immigrants, and foreign countries. I do, however, see his appeal. The incredible level of "PC" we see on a daily basis has crippled free speech in the name of feelings. The gridlock and politically corrupt system begs for a bold and frank business man to straighten D.C. out. But a buffoon such as Trump would completely embarrass our country and ruin our government further.

Hillary Clinton

One does not need to look far to find something rotten in her resume. I think the most telling flaw about her is her incredible lies. Who can forget her bold faced lie about her husband's affair in 1992, her lie about her support for the Iraq war in 2008, the lie about coming under sniper fire in Yugoslavia to name a few. But the more recent lies like her crippling health, confidential email scandal, the Benghazi attacks, and the coordinated DNC attack against Bernie Sanders really tells of Clinton's horrendous personality. It is completely safe to say, she cannot be trusted in or out of public office. If Clinton were to be in office, voters will see more gridlock, more lies, and more conspiracies. Again, I can see why people would vote for her. Clinton is definitely the lesser-of-two-evils and absolutely less threatening than Trump - but her shameless ability to say and lie about anything to get her in office makes her a mystery candidate and, potentially, just as dangerous as Trump.

So what? Why am I writing a cliché post about how bad our candidates are? Well, I feel the compelling need to make at least one post before the first presidential debate. And to the benefit of the reader, I will assume this is all information that you already know. everyone is dreading election day - no matter what you thought of Obama, there is a passing feeling of mourning when imagining seeing Trump or Clinton in his place. No matter who wins, the country will survive, but it is time to vote your conscience and let your voice be heard. In my next post I will write my opinions about my choice candidate (so far). Stay tuned and stay informed

September 23, 2016

I have had a strange urge to promote my pick for 2016 President but have thus far avoided posting because it is all I see. Posts - everywhere - about one of the presidential candidates. And although it really doesn't matter who I choose in my state, I will finally get to it and write my reasons for my presidential candidate.

As I have expressed in my last post, although I have usually voted Republican in the presidential elections, I have seen failure after failure in the candidates chosen and an even bigger failure in social issues. "[Donald Trump] has gotten away with uncountable amounts of ridiculous brain rot - he has convinced normal rational people that he is the only answer". I still love the Republican Party's fiscal responsibility - and I do love Trump's character - but I cannot bring myself to vote for such an erratic and egotistical candidate. I have always voted for the lesser of two evils, but I can't do this any longer.

Hillary Clinton on the other hand is so far from ideal, I bet Bill is having a difficult time voting for her. A completely corrupt and irresponsible liar - [Clinton's] shameless ability to say and lie about anything to get her in office makes her a mystery candidate and, potentially, just as dangerous as Trump. Her record from 1970's until now convinces me, and should convince everyone else that she is a total mystery. Yes, she reveals her plans for office, but it is clear that her plans are not based on her convictions, but rather based on which way the wind blows.

The candidate I am supporting needs to be one that is responsible, clear headed, and has a track record that proves his convictions. In a financial crisis that has been lingering since 2008, the candidate needs to be fiscally conservative - and they need the history to prove it. But, with race and political tension increasing every day, the candidate needs to be socially liberal. Finances do not change - but people do. Which is why our president needs to keep our citizen's liberty in the forefront of their policies.

We need a fiscal Conservative - and a Socially Liberal candidate.

That is why my pick for president is Libertarian candidate Gary Johnson. Here is why:

1) Fiscally Conservative
When Johnson took the office of Governor, New Mexico was in financial turmoil - just like every other state in America. But unlike every state, New Mexico had Johnson. When Governor, Johnson was so set on fixing the financial problem of the state, he vetoed any bill that either couldn't pay for itself, or couldn't be paid for. The number of bills vetoed is 739!

2) Capitalist

Being a true Libertarian, Johnson is a hands-off capitalist. With Johnson, there would be no more unfair and irresponsible government bailouts, "I'm against any type of federal stimulus". This way, the economy is free to do what it does best: make money! In every instance around the world and throughout history: the freer the market, the freer the people.

3) Cutting the budget

Only a truly incompetent voter would suggest that we do not need to cut the budget. Our overwhelming deficit is crippling what little recovery occurs. Johnson, himself, says it best when he first ran for office in 2012 as a Republican, "I have proposed cutting the federal budget by 43 percent to bring it into balance. It can be done. It requires the will and ability to ignore and even fight the special interests that have a vested interest in more and more government spending. Our system is corrupted by special-interest campaign contributions. Crony capitalism permeates our government. The result is that, as the Congressional Budget Office reported this week, the deficit for 2012 will once again exceed $1 trillion"

4) Socially Liberal

Republicans have suffered inconceivable losses in popularity lately by sticking to out-dated, illogical, and biased beliefs - this is not what the Republican party was founded on. If they continue to turn away from the social issues, they turn away from liberty. The issues such as gay marriage, LGBT issues as a whole, religious issues, and views on foreigners take away personal liberties - there is no way around it. If Republicans continue to try and take away choices of individuals, they will cease claims to the idea that they are a party of liberty.

Gary Johnson has shown a deep conviction for personal rights. The idea that the government has no say in our personal decisions is America's most deeply held ideal (or so it used to be). It is time for Americans to realize that personal liberties are personal. If someone thinks they are born with the wrong gender, who am I to try to correct and control that? No matter how odd it may seem.

5) Common Sense Civil Rights

Like the above, Johnson shows a comprehensive understanding for thoughtful civil right actions. Every opinion is no polarized by party lines, but rather by logical thought. On one hand Johnson believes, "Individual liberty includes supporting gay marriage" and on the other hand, "Each state has right to display the Confederate flag." He also believes, "No affirmative action in college admissions nor state jobs" but also supports, "Supports separation of religion and state"

On any issue, Gary Johnson shows a clear understanding for personal liberty and also a Constitution responsibility within our government - both are traits that have been absent from the oval office. The political grid lock, social unrest, and irresponsible government spending is an exact outcome from years of a two-party system merely voting on party lines. If we could just return to a responsible, citizen focused, constitutional nation, then recovery would be all too easy.

Do I think that Gary Johnson will win? It is highly unlikely. But I absolutely cannot vote for either the Republican or Democratic candidate. Johnson, unfortunately, will not be on the first debate stage on Monday, but there is hope! He is not at the 15% mark to land the debate, but if Johnson can capture only 5% of the vote in November, then the Libertarian party could actually receive federal campaign funding - just like the Republican and Democratic party. Either way, I hope my vote can send a message that the two parties are not entitled to our vote.

Whoever you end up voting for - don't settle for the lesser of two evils.

September 25, 2016

What Happened at Wells Fargo?

When one begins their first dead-end job, they learn one thing: management is crazy. Whether it is retail, call centers, fast-food, or maintenance, management is always there breathing down your neck. It is a sign of maturity to ignore these sadistic managers - but they infect far more workplaces than we thought - and it could affect even the customer. At Wells Fargo, we see a great example of perverse management forcing their goals on their inferiors. Here is what actually happened at Wells Fargo.

Upper management at Wells Fargo forced employees to open up unauthorized bank accounts to meet their incredibly unrealistic sales goals. These unauthorized bank accounts were opened up without customer's permission and has been a practice in the company since 2011. CEO John Stumpf has set the goal of 8 accounts per customer because, "8 rhythms with great". You cannot make up a better management fraud story. Since then, over 2 million accounts have been opened for customers.

But that isn't even the worst part: Wells Fargo charged the customers with the fees associated with the accounts! That's right! Not only did upper management tell their employees to commit fraud on a colossal scale, but they charged the customers as well. In response, Stumpf is being chewed out by both the House and the Senate. Wells Fargo has already taken action by firing over 5,300 of their employees. And no: the fired employees were not from management - they were the people opening unauthorized accounts. So the management who ordered the criminal move are not even taking responsibility.

The company thus far is paying $185 million in penalties. But the managers who ordered their employees - at the risk of losing their job - are safe. For now. The next congressional hearing is this Thursday. We can only hope those who encouraged this act and those who did not blow the whistle will receive their justice.

September 26, 2016

The Five Threats of Islam

At the risk of becoming the next Kurt Westergaard, we must declare it and declare it loud that we need to be able to criticize bad ideas and, as Sam Harris put it, "Islam is the mother load of bad ideas. But the criticism of Islam is not only for arguments sake. When one fights Islam ideas, both radical and moderate, you fight for liberty, freedom of speech, and the freedom to simply be happy.

Say what you want about the outspoken, flatulent, controversial, and handsome Milo Yiannopolos, but he has landed in the spotlight on the side of the free man in a way unique to most others. Milo creates a humorous and dubious argument against anyone intolerant of free speech - whether it be the new feminists, social justice warriors, Muslims, and anyone who crosses his path. Milo will simply not tolerate intolerance - as he puts it:

So it gives us a clear answer to the paradox of tolerance: no, you cannot tolerate the truly intolerant. If you give them an inch, they'll take a mile, and rape everything inside it. And they won't stop spreading.

He says this at the University of Central Florida earlier this evening. Despite the Twitter scandal, Milo will not shy away from what most people with a brain thinks: we need free speech in every corner of the world. To protect our happiness and to spread it abroad, the liberty to say whatever we want, without the threat of violence, is absolutely necessary. But no stronger plead for rational discourse than Milo's speech at UCF - just miles away from the Pulse Nightclub. But, although Milo gives amazing reasons to criticize Islam, I think he has given us specific threats Islam poses on the world. And no one is immune. Please let Milo explain as I sum up his points into 5 threats of Islam:

1. The Threat to Women

Because I say things that offend feminists, the left considers me the number one threat to women today. But Muslims do far more than offend feminists, or offend women. They're actually enslaving them, forcing them into marriages, slashing their genitals — which, unlike the male genitalia, aren't improved by a little trim.

Muslims think they own women to such a degree, that they think women who wear shirts above their ankles in European countries are fair game to be raped. That's real rape culture, right there — not the bogus one on college campuses.

So, as long as I'm speaking out against Islam with a louder and more forthright voice than any feminist in America today, I feel justified in considering myself far more feminist than them. Even if I do hate abortion.

2. The Threat to the World

Allah is said to be Compassionate and Merciful, but he does not, in the words of a medieval historian friend of mine, enter into his creation. He does not invite his creatures to be fellow creators. In fact he forbids it. He forbids much of what we in the west know is responsible for all the best art.

He forbids creativity in robust, dangerous, experimental ways. This, I think, rather than any petty sexual restriction, is what means there can be no accommodation made for Islam from gays whatsoever. We are society's engines of chaos, pushing the limits of what can be thought and said, testing the boundaries of creativity and acceptability, sketching out social norms for the rest of you.

The Muslim commander who conquered Alexandria asked the Caliph Umar what to do with the immense library there. According to one anecdote, told by Muslims, the Caliph Umar replied: "If what is written in the books agrees with the Koran, they are not needed. If it disagrees, they are not wanted." So the commander burned the library. Now this may be apocryphal but this story was originally told by Muslims and later repeated by famous Muslim writers.

3. The Threat to Rationality

Curtis Yarvin, a Jewish entrepreneur and blogger, says that nonsense is a better organizing tool than the truth. "Anyone can believe in the truth," he writes. "To believe in nonsense is an unforgivable demonstration of loyalty. It serves as a political uniform."

For many Muslims, the nonsense that is "Islamic science," which holds that the earth is egg-shaped and that the stars are missiles created by Allah to throw at devils, is the only science they need. Or consider the ascendant art of "Islamic creationism," a batty spin on creationist theories forged in Turkey but funded by Saudi Arabia. Scientific inquiry is virtually dead in the Islamic world. Arab nations stand near the bottom of every measure of human development. There is no world-class university anywhere in the Muslim world.

Spain translates more books in a single year than the entire Arab world has in the past thousand. Some people in Saudi Arabia still refuse to believe man has been to the moon. I know some of you tonight probably don't believe we've been to the moon either, but this is America. You are allowed to go against accepted opinion without being beheaded for it.

4. The Threat of Civil Rights

We hear a lot about moderate Muslims, but in practice we don't see them. All the moderate Muslims I know are ex-Muslims, or haven't been to Friday prayers for months, or even years.

London has elected a Muslim mayor, Sadiq Khan, who is praised as a moderate But many have been left wondering just how moderate he is. Khan banned sexy advertisements from the underground like the famous Protein World ads. Was this move really to combat body shaming, like feminists wanted? Or was it to make the underground more shariah-compliant?

It is one of those instances where feminism and Islam are right in line on women's rights. Sadiq Khan has met with a lot of shady and decidedly non-moderate Islamic types. He has associated with convicted terrorist Babar Ahmad, who is credited with inspiring the gang behind the 7/7 bombings. For those of you that don't know, that was London's smaller scale 9/11.

This is a mayor who says terrorism is "Part & parcel of living in a big city" but it shouldn't be, should it? England is one of the most illuminating examples of the lack of moderates. A Gallup poll of Muslims in the UK found that not a single one of the 1,001 people polled thought that homosexuality was morally acceptable. Not a single one!

The entire world loves Malala, the Nobel Prize winning champion of education for girls. But look at her opinion, which passes in the media as moderate: "The more you speak about Islam and against all Muslims, the more terrorists we create." So Malala's opinion is if we all just shut up and did what Islam wants, which is to submit, they wouldn't need to shoot us, stab us, or blow us up. Criticize us and we will kill you for your bad words. Great to know a Nobel prize winner has this sort of vision.

5. The Threat to Law

In 2015 the Center for Security Policy commissioned a poll of Muslims in America. It found that:

- 30% of American Muslims believe it is legitimate to use violence against those that insult Islam
- 25% of American Muslims said that violence against Americans can be justified as part of global jihad
- 51% of American Muslims want to be allowed to be governed by Sharia Law

And here's my personal favorite:

- 33% said that sharia should take precedence over the constitution if they clashed

That's a lot of bad Skittles in the United States. Over a million of them.

Something we can all agree on is that the First Amendment, guaranteeing freedom of speech, is America's most basic right. So it is very telling to understand the opinions of Muslims in America on this topic.

According to a Wenzel Strategies poll in 2012:

- 58% of Muslim-Americans believe criticism of Islam or Muhammad is not protected free speech under the First Amendment
- 45% believe that those who mock Islam should face criminal charges
- 12% believe blaspheming against Islam should be punishable by death

You don't only have to worry about the Muslims who commit acts of terror like shooting up a gay nightclub. You should also be worried about the Muslims who quietly endorse their acts. To say nothing of the ones who fund them.

It is a risk, indeed, to claim that someone's ideas are bad - worse than bad - deadly. Without a doubt, Islam is the worst plague on modern man and it is spreading. The ridiculous notion that we need to simply bend over and accept bad ideas is pure brain rot. Where is the educated and secular Middle East from the early first millennium? It because Islam's first victim.

September 28, 2016

In Defense of "Aleppo Moments"

The number one criticism in the media - and therefore, everyone else - of Gary Johnson is his slip-ups in recent interviews. The most revealing part about this publicity is that Mr. Johnson has so little to attack. The fact that the media picks these self-proclaimed "Aleppo Moments" should be a good thing. Those who choose to bring up his slip-ups in casual debates just proves that they really have no idea who Gary Johnson is.

Mike Barnicle, the MSNBC commentator of the Morning Joe program had Libertarian Candidate Gary Johnson on for a casual interview. The interview was mostly unwatched except for when Barnicle asked Johnson how he would address the refugee crisis in Aleppo to which he responded, "What is Aleppo?" After some explaining from Barnicle, Johnson responded that the United States must respond with a coalition to improve the situation there.

Now, on its surface, it does seem like a pretty big mistake. To the simple minded, it would appear Johnson is an airhead who does not know foreign policy basics. But when the conversation arises, I challenge you to ask the accuser to point out Aleppo on the world map. Chances are, they can't do it. The most outstanding point one could hear is that Aleppo is the Syrian Capital (In fact, there are multiple Aleppo's in Syria alone). This just proves they do not know what they are talking about. Aleppo is simply the major city in the heat of the Syrian Civil war (the capital is actually Damascus).

The other and more recent mess up was also on MSNBC when Chris Matthews, hosting the town hall meeting, asked Johnson to name his favorite foreign leader, or any foreign leader he admires. Again, those with a small attention span will proclaim, "Johnson doesn't know any foreign leaders!" Some people can be so small minded.

Matthews continued when Johnson couldn't think of an answer, "Go ahead, you gotta do this. Anywhere. Any continent. Canada, Mexico, Europe, over there, Asia, South America, Africa. Name a foreign leader that you respect."

Now, keep in mind that Johnson is a Libertarian - typically very skeptical of authority. The lack of an answer was simply due to the fact that Johnson probably does not idolize any living leader. Everyone has their faults and that was what Johnson was probably stuck on. He ended up saying, "I guess I'm having an Aleppo moment in thinking of the name of the former president of Mexico" Luckily, Libertarian Vice-presidential candidate Bill Weld clarified, "Vicente Fox". The video is below:

Again, the best defense one can use is to turn the question and ask, "who is your favorite foreign leader that you admire?" Most likely, they can't name one. I honestly can't name a living foreign leader I admire and Johnson responded recently by saying, "It's been almost 24 hours...and I still can't come up with a foreign leader I look up to"

I would love to hear Trump or Clinton's response to this. Maybe they'd say Putin? I appeal to the fair mindedness of the readers and assume you are of above average intelligence, and I still think these questions would be difficult to answer.

Watch the interview and make your decision and remember: this slip-up is the worst the media has on Johnson - whereas Trump/Clinton have a lifetime of these "Aleppo Moments"

September 29, 2016

Letters to a Young Contrarian [Book Review]

There are very few books that earn a place on my bookshelf. I have 3 bookshelfs, but I have one shelf that hangs right over my desk that holds my absolute favorite, thought-provoking books. Even then, there are some that seem to stand out - but none can match Letters to a Young Contrarian by Christopher Hitchens. Published back in 2001, Letters is a relatively new book, but within its pages it holds a beautifully written series of letters that are so profound - they will stand out as a truly philosophically outstanding work.

Letters to a Young Contrarian is a play on the book Letters to a Young Poet by Rainer Maria Rilke - and just like Rilke included letters written to 19 year old Franz Kappus, Hitchens includes letters written to a fictional character (the reader) that perfectly encapsulates his indignation and intellect that he wishes to impart on the reader. Hitchens gracefully touches on a variety of issues from familiar territory such as religion, morality, government, and liberty to lesser known stories and facts ranging from Nathaniel Hawthorne to even Josef Goebbels. It seems a daunting task to summarize the value of this book - but having have read and reread and rereread this work, I feel compelled to say something. Like all good works, there are pencil marks on just about every page with notes. From that, I have compiled some of the greatest lesson from each letter - so allow me the vain pleasure of taking it upon myself to summarize just a few of the lessons from this outstanding compilation.

"...when the celebrity culture and the spin-scum and the crooked lawyers and the pseudo-statesmen and the clerics seemed to have everything their own way. they will be back, of course. They will always be "back". They never leave."

Here, even in the preface of Hitchens works, we have amazing insights. This one, however, is something of a warning. The fight for liberty and independent thinking is a constant one. It is generation by generation, decade by decade, and year by year. In the first letter he expands on the 'fight' be introducing the reader (who Hitch refers to as "My Dear X") by speaking about basic contrarian arguments but ends the chapter with an important lesson:

"To be in opposition is not to be a nihilist. And there is no decent or charted way of making a living at it. It is something you are, and not something you do."

It is a play on what Hitchens has been saying for years. I even have one remark on the cover image of this page, "The essence of an independent mind lies not in what it thinks, but in how it thinks". It almost seems like a whole new enlightenment when one becomes an independent thinker - to know that you will never go back. it is a beautiful thing.

"It's for this reason that I am quite sure of two thins. The first is that even uneducated people...have an innate capacity to resist and, if not even to think for themselves, to have thoughts occur to them... the second is that we do not naturally aspire to any hazy, narcotic Nirvana, where our critical and ironic faculties would be of no use to use."

Again, expanding on his first point, Hitchens reminds us that independent thinking is not popular nor natural. He expands on that by pointing to the Bible with a witty jab, "Imagine a state of endless praise and gratitude and adoration, as the Testaments ceaselessly enjoin us to do, and you have conjured a world of hellish nullity and conformism." Hitch actually warns against those who absolutely think they are right. Just this lesson alone would benefit the world in a way that could only be compared to the invention of the printing press.

"I suggest you learn to recognize and avoid symptoms of the zealot and the person who knows that he is right"

In the next few letters, we see more dissecting into illogical thinking patterns. The "decline of intellectual and moral standards" is completely explained and trashed by Hitch:

"They want god on their side and believe they are doing his work - what is this, even at its very best, but an extreme for of solipsism? They are from conclusion to evidence; our greatest resource is the mind, and the mind is not well-trained by being taught to assume what has to be proved."

He has always been one to say that it is not to want to act against illogical irrational actions, but to have to act - and I think that ideal sums up his works as a whole:

"Allow a friend to believe in a bogus prospectus or a false promise and you cease, after a short while, to be a friend at all. How dare you intervene? As well ask, How dare you not?"

This compilation is only 141 pages long, but holds thoughts and ideas that are completely ahead of its time. Hitchens outlines the independent mind, dangerous thinkers, and conformist warnings that provides the reader with invaluable life lessons. I could write multiple articles about this book if I could! But to keep this under 1000 words, let me finish with one more quote (because any article about Christopher Hitchens is often filled with quotes):

"...everybody can do something, and that the role of dissident is not, and should not be, a claim of membership in a communion of saints...And of course, one never has to worry about there being a surplus of such people. Those who need or want to think for themselves will always be a minority..."

September 30, 2016

October 2016

Referendum in Hungary

Hungary surprised many around the world last year when the tiny Eastern European country decided to take migrant issues into their own hands by constructing a huge fence along their southern border. By doing so, they actually diverted migrants passed their own country and to more Northern and far more wealthy countries – but have worsened relations with other European Union countries.

Hungarian Prime Minister Vikto Orban believes that the loss of relations with the North is worth it because he has kept out migrants and terrorism, "The more migrants there are, the greater the risk of terror" Orban, who sees himself as a hero to the Hungarian people now needs to stand against the EU itself to keep these anti-immigration policies implemented. Late last year, the European Union created a migration plan that would allow more migrants into the continent and make it easier to relocate. The plan meant to make Greece and Italy (the biggest entry points) accept more migrants – but it puts huge strains on smaller countries like Greece, Croatia, and other Balkan countries, including Hungary.

Unlike Germany and Sweaden, Hungary does not have the economy to support additional migrants nor is it prepared to. The biggest problem with the EU plan is that many countries see the Union as an authoritarian bully. Mr. Orban has spoken out about this before calling the EU "unelected, liberal elite" And although Orban's policies are unpopular globally, they are extremely popular in Hungary. His "Fidesz" party actually saw a huge increase in voters and more support from other parties like the Jobbik Party – which is a significant tactical advantage for Orban's next move against the EU demands: another referendum.

Yes, another one! It seems that, along with the United Kingdom, other countries wish to have their voices and concerns heard – and this migration crisis is the boiling point. The Hungarian voters will answer the question: "Do you want the European Union to be able to mandate the obligatory resettlement of non-Hungarian citizens into Hungary even without the approval of the National Assembly?" At this point in time, there seems to be large support of a "No" vote on the referendum due to Orban's success.

Two days ago, Orban described the migration plan as illegal and unreasonable and "If there are more 'no' votes than 'yes' votes, that means Hungarians do not accept the rule which the bureaucrats of the European Commission want to forcefully impose on us." Even though Orban seems to have odd reasons for opposing migrants, namely the "dilution of European Christian culture", he does stand up for his country in a crisis that the Hungarian people are weary of. The bottom line is: a sovereign nation needs a voice – and we have seen little room negotiations within the EU.

October 2, 2016

Colombia votes "no"!

The 1940's was littered with death and war – of which South America was not immune to. Despite America's promised protection of the South American countries through the Monroe Doctrine, Fascist and Communist influence still seeped its way into the jungles and mountains of the isolated corner of the world. Falangism and Hispanidad began its career in South America and infected Bolivia, Brazil, Chile, Paraguay, Uruguay, Venezuela, and of course, Colombia. The tensions on conflicting Communist and Fascist forces met a flash point when Jorge Elicer Gaitan was assassinated forcing the leading Conservative and Liberal party to join forces and issued a "Declaration of Sitges" and formed what they called a "National Front". Out of the ashes of the anti-government and anti-fascist regimes which have claimed over 200,000 peasant lives in Colombia in what is now known as La Violencia, the "FARC" is born.

The Revolutionary Armed Forces of Colombia – People's Army was formed in 1964 and was backed by Cuba, the Soviet Union, and the Irish Republican Army among other Communist allies. Utilizing their jungle homeland, the FARC was primarily a guerrilla movement, but has also been involved with kidnapping and drug trading to fund their movement. Just like any typical Communist movement, FARC fought against the aggression and capitalistic expansions of the Colombian government. The largest advancement of the FARC was in the 1980's when they changed their strategy to more militaristic and rural combat. With money from a coca boom, FARC began sending troops to the Soviet Union and Vietnam to receive more advanced training. Since these rural attacks, peace talks continued throughout the 80's and 90's with little success. Lack of communication made cease-fires impossible.

Fighting picked up and tensions rose even more in the 90's and 2000's when both sides began to become even more coordinated and brutal. Former president Alvaro Uribe made huge attacks against the group and FARC in return, increased it's attacks on civilian centers. The Colombian citizens could not stand the group anymore and produced several anti-FARC rallies and pressured the government to end the conflict. Finally, in 2008, FARC leaders began dying and even Hugo Chavez called the group to stand down – but to no avail.

It wasn't until earlier this week that President Santos and FARC leader Rodrigo Londono actually came close to a peace treaty. Signed with a pen made from recycled bullets, the two leaders struck a deal that would end the 50 year war and give FARC more of a say in the Colombian government, and although the President was completely on board with the deal, the Colombian people were not. Due to the generation long struggle with murder, crime, and extortion, the referendum vote for the peace deal failed – by just .23%! A total of 50.22% of voters did not agree to give FARC a say in the government even if it means peace. Unlike President Santos, the barbaric murder and kidnappings are still in the minds of the victims – and they have chosen not to accept FARC's crimes to become a ticket to power.

Luckily, the cease fire will stay in place and peace talks will resume in Havana, Cuba – but we have seen an honorable display of integrity and a responsible democratic vote in the heat of a war torn country. Both sides want peace – but not at the expense of a generation of murder, kidnapping, and crime.

October 4, 2016

Kaine VS. Pence

The Clinton – Kaine team made it no secret that the debate will be focused around offense toward Trump and Pence – and it shows! I was completely skeptical about this debate following the boring, peaceful first presidential debate – but I was wrong! Kaine came out in a fiery offensive aimed at Trump and Pence was calmly ready for the attack. If you have seen my past posts about Mike Pence specifically, I was not too nice. Pence has supported anti-science and anti-rational legislation throughout his career. But, with Kaine's aimless and naive attacks, Pence has been revealed to be more collected and knowledgeable than Kaine, Clinton, and even Trump!

Tim Kaine, senator from Virginia has shown the public how desperate the campaign is a this point. Even though the Clinton team is actually ahead in the key swing states, the horrendously disrespectful and childish performance by Kaine really makes me doubt that the margins will stay so distant. Mike Pence, however, did prove to be the bigger man by keeping a calm head in the 72 times he and the moderator was interrupted by Kaine. The moderator of the event, CBS reporter Elaine Quijano, however, failed to keep a lid on Kaine's hot head – making the debate humorously difficult to watch. Each time Pence tried to answer or defend a claim, Kaine brought out another attack before he could finish. Pence responded, "If you could let me answer I can get to these one at a time" – Of course, Kaine didn't let him finish by challenging Pence to defend Trump's record...again!

Of course, interruptions do not make someone a bad presidential candidate – I am reminded that even cool-headed Obama was one to interrupt sometimes. But there is something to be said about a grown adult who cannot allow their contestant to finish a sentence – and then imagine those same people trying to function in the U.S. Senate! Let me add my favorite crosstalk from the debate. When asked to defend the idea that many voters see Trump as a risky choice, Pence responded to Kaine's claims about Hillary:

...I mean, the situation we're watching hour by hour in Syria today is the result of the failed foreign policy and the weak foreign policy that Hillary Clinton helped lead in this administration and create. The newly emboldened — the aggression of Russia, whether it was in Ukraine or now they're heavy-handed approach...
[INTERRUPTION]

KAINE: You guys love Russia. You both have said...

PENCE: ... their heavy-handed approach [INTERRUPTION]

KAINE: You both have said — you both have said Vladimir Putin is a better leader than the president.

PENCE: Well...[INTERRUPTION]

QUIJANO: Well, we're going to get to Russia in just a moment. But I do want to get back to the question at...

PENCE: But in the midst — Elaine, thank you. Thank you. Thank you, Senator, I'll...[INTERRUPTION]

KAINE: These guys have praised Vladimir Putin as a great leader. How can that...[INTERRUPTION]

QUIJANO: Yes, and we will get to that, Senator. We do have that coming up here. But in the meantime, the questions...[INTERRUPTION]

PENCE: Well, Senator, I must have hit a...[INTERRUPTION]

PENCE: I must have hit a nerve here.

QUIJANO: Why the disconnect?

Pence: ... Look, to get to your question about trustworthiness, Donald Trump has built a business through hard times and through good times. He's brought an extraordinary business acumen. He's employed tens of thousands of people in this country [INTERRUPTION]

KAINE: You are Donald Trump's apprentice. Let me talk about this...[INTERRUPTION]

PENCE: Senator, I think I'm still on my time. [INTERRUPTION]

KAINE: Well, I think — isn't this a discussion?

QUIJANO: This is our open discussion.

KAINE: Yeah, let's talk about the state of...[INTERRUPTION]

PENCE: Well, let me interrupt — let me interrupt you and finish my sentence, if I can.

KAINE: Finish your sentence.

PENCE: The Clinton Foundation accepted foreign contributions from foreign governments and foreign donors while she was secretary of state [INTERRUPTION]

KAINE: OK, now I can weigh in. Now...

PENCE: She had a private server...[INTERRUPTION]

KAINE: Now, I get to weigh in. Now, let me just say this...[INTERRUPTION]

PENCE: ... that was discovered...[INTERRUPTION]

QUIJANO: ... Senator, you have an opportunity to respond.

PENCE: ... keep that pay to play process out of the reach of the public.

KAINE: Governor Pence — Governor Pence doesn't think the world's going so well and he, you know, is going to say it's everybody's fault.

PENCE: Do you?

And so it goes. If you are weary of either candidate and politics as a whole, you might not like this debate. If you do not like either candidate, like the situation I found myself in, you will see presidential Pence vs a desperate Kaine. So far I have written two posts regarding Pence's credulity – but it seems I need to begin digging into Kaine's past – no doubt I will find similarly childish and naive instances in his past.

October 5, 2016

Trump's Tax Return
_____

A lot of talk has been spreading about Trump's leaked tax return – most of which is incorrect. Tax preparers around America must be pulling out their hair over the amount of misinformation. The return was recently leaked by an anonymous source and published by the New York Times. The return revealed a few pages from a tax return from 1995 with "The Trump Foundation" at the top of the page. After the return proved legitimate, attacks began to fire from all directions! From Clinton, the Washington post, and many so-called professionals – but their claims only reveal how little they know.

The biggest controversy is with the bottom line of the return showing a 9 hundred million dollar loss for the year. Losses are a normal part of doing business – clients take losses every year! It is as normal as taking tax credits. Even Steve Jobs had a loss of just over 1 billion dollars before he died – but unlike Steve Jobs, Donald Trump is being labeled a crook, a criminal, and a bad businessman. Why? Because the accusers have no idea what they are talking about. Let me explain.

When a business has a loss for the year, they can write off that amount to lower their income for the year. If the amount is greater than the amount of income earned, you are limited to the amount you lost, so to write off the remainder amount, the IRS allows you to carry the amount forward 20 years. For example, let's say my dog, Tax, is in business and losses $500 one year. Next year, Tax makes $250 in business – he can now carry forward the $500 from last year to eliminate the income. And so on until the loss is eliminated or the 20-year mark is met. (1)

Kind of confusing until you write it out on paper. The IRS Publication 536 spells out exactly the same rules I wrote above. Again, it is important to know that people do this all the time. (2) If they couldn't, then an incredible amount of small businesses would vanish. So the idea that taking the loss is a loophole in the tax code is completely false – regardless if you like Trump or not. It is not a loophole, it is not fraud, it is not irresponsible. Keep in mind that Trump had hundreds of thousands of stakeholders including employees. Investors, suppliers, financiers, and other third-party vendors. In the business world, we call this a "fiduciary duty". He not only needs to look after himself, but also look after his stakeholders. (3)

The claim that Trump did not pay income taxes for most of the past few decades is true. We don't have all of his return just yet, but it is safe to say that with a huge loss, no income taxes are paid. Eric Trump even declared that he did not pay income taxes. But what most do not know is that business owners pay so much more tax than just income tax. Every paycheck employers must pay additional FICA and other payroll taxes in addition to employee taxes. They also pay a tremendous amount of city and state taxes as well as provide many people jobs to pay taxes.

To say that Trump's taxes are fraudulent is to admit you don't know what you are talking about

October 6, 2016

Chess Master Nazi Paikidze Standing up for Liberty

When a brave soul stands up against injustices, we rarely hear about it – what is even more rare, is when someone stands up against Iran. Well, both has happened recently with the World champion Women's Chess tournament in Iran. Nazi Paikidze hold the international Master and Woman Grandmaster titles and has become Junior champion multiple times in her youth. Needless to say, this Georgian – American is an incredibly brilliant young woman – but her rational mind does not stay on the chess table.

Iran has been chosen as the 2017 location to host the Women's Chess World Championship – Both chess and women are an unusual find in the country. And by law, women must legally wear at least a hijab or a headscarf. Paididze decided that she will not wear the hijab and thinks "…it's unacceptable to host a women's World Championship in a place where women do not have basic fundamental rights and are treated as second-class citizens." Because of this crazy requirement, Nazi is boycotting the event and has made a petition for others to do the same thing, "I am not anti-Islam or any other religion. I stand for freedom of religion and choice," she says, "I'm protesting FIDE's [the world chess federation] decision not because of Iran's religion or people, but for the government's laws that are restricting my rights as a woman."

Standing up to the regime of intolerance toward their own women and foreign women has not gone without it's own backfire. The women's committee of international chess governing body, Susan Polgar, tried to keep Nazi quite by advising her to keep her opinions off of Twitter. She responded, "I already did. Thanks to Twitter this issue got a lot of attention as well." To which Polgar responded, "Not the right position to insult me and members of @WOMChess when we are trying to help you" Showing the same poise and professionalism, Nazi showed no fear responding, "Nothing of what I said was a personal insult/attack to anyone but FIDE's decision."

It is a defining characteristic of oppression when a totalitarian regime forces their own citizen's compliance – and also believes everyone else's citizens must do the same. In this situation, they received resistance! No doubt in the name of women around the world – but specifically for Iranian women. In the past, women have complied without resistance – Karika Dronavalli, an Indian chess master tried to explain, "For a few days it was a bit awkward to play with the headscarf, but slowly I got used to it. I feel we need to respect their culture and customs." This show for respect is a two way street, Miss Dronavalli – and oppression will not stop until we see more brave people stand up like Nazi Paikidze.

October 6, 2016

Joshua Wong: Freedom Fighter

Citizens in the West are far luckier than they realize. We hear about the struggles for basic freedoms that are taken for granted. It is absolutely necessary to focus on the struggles abroad to remind ourselves how fortunate we really are. Perhaps if news reports show these struggles for Democracy, then we could support our foreign comrades – the harsh reality of the life of freedom fighters could force the American public to abandon petty social justice fights and join together to fight for those around the world.

I bring this up because of the amazing power of China to oppose Democracy even outside of their borders! Joshua Wong is a young student leader best known for the pro – Democracy movement he was involved with in Hong Kong back in 2014. But hostilities against the young protester are not limited to China's borders. Mr. Wong was on his way to Bangkok from Hong Kong on Wednesday to participate in a debate of students on the 40th Anniversary of the Thammasart Massacre. A fitting event that Wong visit an event that featured protests against a dictator by students who were actually murdered. When he arrived in Bangkok, his passport was taken and he was quickly deported back to Hong Kong after spending ten hour being illegally detained. According to Thailand's student activist group the "New Democracy Movement", the detention of Joshua Wong was due to a letter China sent out. It appears that China is keeping tabs on their students and even demanding their neighboring allies to do the same. China defended the accusation saying that they, "...respects Thai immigration policy, and did not respond to inquiries regarding the existence of a letter..." China does very little to protect the rights of their citizens, and students like Wong, are especially in danger seeing as they cannot even leave their own country.

Many supporters were extremely worried about Wong being detained. It is no secret that pro-Democracy protesters mysteriously go missing. In the past, many authors and booksellers have gone missing only to return "reformed". Chinese and foreign people have gone missing such as Lee Bo (British Citizen), Gui Minhai (Swedish Citizen), Lui Bo, Lam Wing-kee, and Cheung Jiping to name a few. Luckily, Wong did make it back to Hong Kong – whether that is better or worse than Bangkok is up to Chinese officials. Stories like these are drowned out by petty social justice warriors and election drama – but if the West truly cares about Democracy world-wide, more attention is demanded.

"I'm not scared, because I know that I need to face the trial. What I mean is, I already expect I will need to pay the price...We are not seeking revolution. We just want democracy!" – Joshua Wong

October 8, 2016

Did Glenn Beck Endorse Hillary Clinton?

After Beck's falling out with the Republican party and the youth, the failed Ted Cruz endorsement and the failed religious credulity, no rational person really respects Glenn Beck's opinions – but something happened today that seems like Beck has taken yet another step toward insanity: endorsing Hillary Clinton... maybe.

Many news outlets are reporting the shocking statement Glenn Beck made today regarding moral voting in the upcoming election. In a Facebook post, Beck says:

"Every person, each of us must decide what is a bridge too far... It is not acceptable to ask a moral, dignified man to cast his vote to help elect an immoral man who is absent decency or dignity. If the consequence of standing against Trump and for principles is indeed the election of Hillary Clinton, so be it. At least it is a moral, ethical choice." (1)

There is no one left in America who Glenn Beck has not surprised. Glenn Beck has been Never Trump since the beginning – and for good reasons. I definitely do not support or endorse Donald Trump either, but the lifetime of Conservative reporting and support would make anyone assume Beck would grudgingly vote for Trump like the rest of the Republican party. (2) But it seems like a lapse of judgment made Beck go just a little too far because the sun didn't even set on the Facebook post when he was asked to clarify and he responded on Vice and his website that:

"I Am Neither Endorsing Nor Voting for Hillary Clinton" (3)

Vice News, and everyone else on Earth thought that it was something of an endorsement. Beck is completely against the lesser-of-two-evils vote (ignoring his own voting record) but he does admit to the fallacy that not voting for Trump means Hillary will win. Going further, he even admits that Hillary, even with his 30 year-old stance against her, is a moral and ethical choice.

Listening to Beck is like listening to a dementia patient: nothing is certain, proof is unnecessary, and the points are mute. This dementia-like move from Beck could be just a cry for attention – like many of his statements lately, but he definitely didn't mean what he said. YES – it sounded like an endorsement but NO – Glenn Beck didn't mean to endorse Hillary.

October 11, 2016

What Happened at Wells Fargo? [Update]

A few weeks ago, I posted about the Wells Fargo scandal where upper management directed their employees to fraudulently open customer accounts. These unauthorized bank accounts were opened up without customer's permission and has been a practice in the company since 2011. CEO John Stumpf has set the goal of 8 accounts per customer because, "8 rhythms with great". You cannot make up a better management fraud story. Since then, over 2 million accounts have been opened for customers.

John Stumpf has taken over this scandal and has reported to congressional meetings that have been investigating the issue. So far, Wells Fargo paid $185 Million in fines and have fired over 5,300 employees – keep in mind that the employees fired were not managers in anyway. The ones who made the decision and enforced the "8 accounts per customer" rule and punished the employees for not going along with their scam got off free!

Luckily, the aging slimy CEO Stumpf has finally submitted his resignation after dealing with the scandal – effectively taking the blame for the issue. (1) John Stumpf is not receiving any severance from Wells Fargo – maybe he was getting tired of scamming people. He is, however, leaving with more than $100 million in vested stock, plus accumulated pension and 401(k) benefits exceeding $24 million. (2)

The issue does seem to be settled. The employees who were fired or quit because they were forced to comply with the Fargo scam are taking action against the company, who will probably bow to their demands. The company did step into the slimy fraudulent lime light for a brief second, but, purging Stumpf without severance seems to be a great way to get over this and try to start new.

October 12, 2016

No One Left to Lie To

Now, when someone talks about Hillary Clinton, they usually think "Presidential Candidate" or "Former Secretary of State" or "Former Senator" – but just a slight glance at her 30 year record will make you think "fraud" or "robotic liar" or "ruthless bully". Here are some of the many lies that makes Hillary a irredeemable, deplorable candidate – but I guess when everyone ignores her past – at this point, what difference does it make?

- Lied about ignoring the rules for handling of sensitive national security information
- Benghazi
- Amassed a personal fortune with "speaking fees"
- Said she left the White House in debt
- Claimed that she never ran a negative ad against Bernie
- Payments from private sector political donors and foreign governments
- Flunked the D.C. Bar Exam
- Lied about Pence cutting the education budget in Illinois
- Claimed that all her grandparents being immigrants
- Lied about being named after Sir Edmond Hillary
- Lied about a "vast right-wing conspiracy" that led to the impeachment Bill Clinton
- The Whitewater scandal
- Lied about being denied by the Marines in 1975
- Lied to cover up her husband's infidelity
- Lied about "sniper fire" in Bosnia
- Claimed Solar has more jobs than Oil
- Claimed every bill she passed had a Republican co-signer
- Claimed Bill Clinton got 100 times more people out of poverty than Ronald Reagan
- Said she was against the Iraq war before Obama

October 13, 2016

Rudy Giuliani Lies about Clinton

There seems to be a mysterious brain rot spreading on the 2016 election campaign trail – and it seems former New York mayor, Rudy Giuliani is no exception. Last week, Giuliani was plugging for Trump at a rally in Ocala, Florida when his seemingly aged brain slipped into a brow-raising tirade against Hillary Clinton. Clinton and Giuliani both served the Empire State in the early millennia and both were at Ground Zero on September 11, 2001 – but not according to Mr. Giuliani. (1) The senior moment began with Rudy spouting off an outrageous claim that Hillary was not even at Ground Zero:

"Don't tell me, if you said that, that you remember Sept. 11, 2001. I remember Sept. 11, 2001. Yes, yes, you helped to get benefits for the people that were injured that day. But I heard her say one day she was there that day. I was there that day. I don't remember seeing Hillary Clinton there. That was like when she said she had to run through gunfire. That turned out to be, what do we call it? A lie."

In what can only be a brain-rotting senior moment, Giuliani makes a humorous remark about Clinton's infamous Bosnian lie. It could have been a great attack – if only it were true. Almost instantly, photos of the two New York public servants together at Ground Zero surfaced.

Is this a single, irresponsible, unintelligible slip up? Or has "America's Mayor" lost his mind. It is very possible that the mayor is really this absent minded – the Trump slip ups don't confine themselves to that toupee. Giuliani apologized for the accusation soon after the photo surfaced, however, *"I made a mistake. I'm wrong and I apologize"* (2)

This is not his only crazy moments. The 2016 election has infected the mayor — and his remarks make that apparent. Many people who have spoke with him have spoke with him recently. Reporter Rachel Maddow remarked, "[he] seems nuts!" Stephen Colbert refers to him as, "the former Rudy Giuliani". It is true, that the hero America saw on the rubble of the World Trade Center is gone – infected by the rat race of this election. Insisting that the dead will vote for the Democrats. (3) Whether it be a depressing shamble – or a knee slapping freak show, please keep in mind that these people on the campaign trail really believe what they say.

October 18, 2016

Predicting the Presidential Election

With the election day looming around the corner, predictions are all over the place as far as who will win this November. The majority of the polls and experts suggest that Hillary will win, but this is an election like we have never seen before. The U.S. is torn between two of the least favorable candidates in history, a flamboyant tough guy and a chronic liar – the ticket could not be harder to predict. The unprecedented independent candidate success plays into the uncertainty as much as the voters who choose to sit this election out. All of this casts a huge fog over the nation as to what will happen this November – however, one professor thinks he has the answer.

Dr. Allan Lichtman is a professor of history at American university and has created a formula to predict the results of U.S. Presidential elections – and he has proven the formula correct by accurately predicting the elections since 1984! (1) In Litchman's book, "Predicting the Next President: The Keys to the White House 2016", he has laid out several true/ false questions to determine the victor – the guidelines are as follows:

- **Party Mandate:** After the midterm elections, the incumbent party holds more seats in the U.S. House of Representatives than after the previous midterm elections.
- **Contest:** There is no serious contest for the incumbent party nomination.
- **Incumbency:** The incumbent party candidate is the sitting president.
- **Third party:** There is no significant third party or independent campaign.
- **Short-term economy:** The economy is not in recession during the election campaign.
- **Long-term economy:** Real per capita economic growth during the term equals or exceeds mean growth during the previous two terms.
- **Policy change:** The incumbent administration effects major changes in national policy.
- **Social unrest:** There is no sustained social unrest during the term.
- **Scandal:** The incumbent administration is untainted by major scandal.
- **Foreign/military failure:** The incumbent administration suffers no major failure in foreign or military affairs.
- **Foreign/military success:** The incumbent administration achieves a major success in foreign or military affairs.
- **Incumbent charisma:** The incumbent party candidate is charismatic or a national hero.
- **Challenger charisma:** The challenging party candidate is not charismatic or a national hero.

The keys are 13 true/false questions, where an answer of "true" always favors the reelection of the party holding the White House. After answering these questions, Litchman admitted this is an incredibly hard election to predict but he has decided to make the prediction that Trump will be the victor this year. How can that be? He made the prediction about a month ago before the leaked sound bite about grabbing women – but the professor sticks by it.

It is hard to say if that is wise or not. There are at least some shreds of evidence to suggest that the news channels and some polling to be eschewed against Trump – so it is not impossible. This could be, as David Cameron suggested, Trump will "be the new Ronald Reagan" (2). Just like the Brexit vote in the UK earlier this year, the US presidential election may not have been polled accurately. Either way, it will be close. I will submit my own presidential prediction after tonight's debate.

The best part about hating both candidates is you truly get to enjoy the attacks from both sides. After this debate, I will make an attempt at making a state-by-state prediction of my own – so stay tuned.

October 19, 2016

My 2016 Presidential Election Prediction [Part 1]

In a gambling type of pleasure, I really want to make an election prediction. Having the least two favorable candidates in history surely doesn't help, and the unpredictable leaks makes predicting this election all the more unstable. Of course, hindsight is going to be 20-20, but as for now, it is kind of hard to tell how this election will turn out. I actually have been keeping up with the polls and think that it would be a great time to make a guess. I Tried to publish this prediction before the last debate, but after the trump and Hillary leaks, it was not wise to assume the results were even close to predictable.

For my prediction, I will include a map of each state and I will break the states down into groups: Solid States, Swing States, and Independent States. Here is my first prediction, subject to change after the first debate:

SOLID STATES

Most of these are pretty obvious and most consider these states to not be in play in this election, and sometimes, ever. For Donald trump and the Republican states, we have Idaho, Minnesota, Wyoming, North Dakota, South Dakota, Nebraska, Kansas, Oklahoma, Texas, Arkansas, Louisiana, Alaska, Mississippi, Missouri, Tennessee, Alabama, Georgia, South Carolina, Kentucky and West Virginia. AS far as Hillary Clinton and the Democrat states, I expect these states too will fall along the usual states such as Washington, Oregon, California, Colorado, Hawaii, Wisconsin, Illinois, Michigan, Pennsylvania, New York, New Jersey, Rhode Island, Connecticut, New Hampshire, Vermont, and Maine. There will be no doubt as to these states.

SWING STATES

The real states that matter are the swing states. Most are the typical states such as Iowa, Ohio, Virginia, Florida, and North Carolina. Others would usually include New Hampshire and Minnesota due to the Republican leadership there, but Clinton is seeing large leads there so I consider those two hers. However, despite Trumps recent gaffs, he does hold a decent lead in Iowa and Ohio. Even though it is close in these states, I am willing to guess the results.

Iowa, and Ohio will go to Trump. The leads in North Carolina are in favor of Clinton, but I expect Trump to win one of these swing states – probably North Carolina. Pennsylvania, usually a state-in-play, is Clinton's for sure. The big states like Virginia and Florida, however close, will also go to her. The states that will win it for her are Pennsylvania, Florida, and Virginia.

INDEPENDENT STATES

Consistent readers of mine will know that I am somewhat grudgingly voting for Johnson just to make my vain, futile attempt to fight the two-party system. If it works or not, Independent Candidates are making a huge impact nationwide. Of course there is Johnson and Stein holding onto their 8% and 2% votes, respectively. But there is also presidential candidate McMullen in Utah making huge leads in that state that could tip the scale away from trump and Clinton.

In Utah, Clinton and Trump have 25.5% and 31.8% respectively, but a recent surge brought McMullen up to 22.8% in that state over the course of two weeks! Whether he wins that state or not, McMullen is a surprising new twist in that state in particular – and whether we should expect more from him, or the other independent candidates will remain to be seen. As of now, it would not matter too much in the election as a whole – but it may loosen the two-party grip.

The only other two states that I would assign to this are New Mexico and Alaska which have shown big independent support recently. New Mexico, Johnson's former state is a victory for Clinton with 40% for her and only 20% for Johnson. Alaska, too has seen gains for Johnson, but have predictable fallen considerably since his Aleppo gaffs. Either way, Independent candidates are making unprecedented success nationwide that can, hopefully, help reject the two party system that has, up till now, failed to represent us.

October 19, 2016

My 2016 Election Prediction [Part 2]

Earlier last month, I made the naive decision to make some election predictions. Absolutely hating both candidates, like most voters do this election, I think I have an unbiased view on the results. But even with that, these two candidates are impossible to predict. Immediately after my first prediction, Trump had some lewd comments leak, Clinton had even more emails released, women pressed rape charges against Trump, and the FBI investigation showed signs of re-opening. Because of that, I think my previous prediction is now void.

Following a few poll averaging, I decide that the main state to watch is Florida. Following Clinton's relationship with the FBI, the polls swing "big league" in Trump's favor. Now, it sits at a close tie – but the big change seems to suggest that Trump has a bigger elad there than we thought. In my newest prediction Florida and New Hampshire are the only ones I really changed. And although the polls swing back and forth in most swing states, I believe they will stay as they are. Here is my new electoral map showing an ominous result:

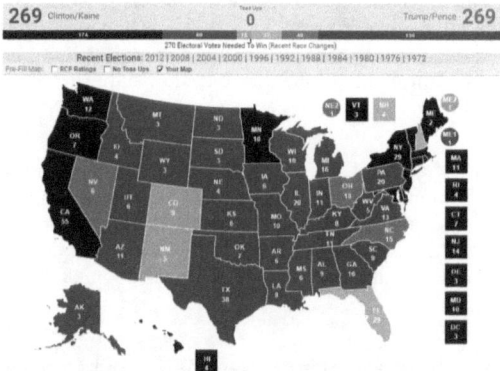

I do think that Clinton will ultimately win this election, but there is nowhere on this map I think could change in a big enough way to stand by. Based on the trend as a whole, this map seems to be a s accurate as I can get. There must be one or two states that will surprise us to show a Clinton victory – but that remains to be seen. Either way, election night will be a dubious and thrilling night. Be sure to tune in and avoid any riots.

November 7, 2016

Trump at Gettysburg

Mirroring the Republican Party's founder, Donald Trump made an amazing speech yesterday that reminded the voters why he is running in the first place – and more importantly, why so many voters are drawn to him. Donald Trump, rallying his supporters up, summoned rekindled passions pleading them to, "to rise above the noise and the clutter of our broken politics, and to embrace that great faith and optimism that has always been the central ingredient in the American character"

In the surprisingly sober and well-spoken speech, Donald Trump proposed a contract with the voters and the American people. Trump plays on another historical party moment when, in 1994, Newt Gingrich and the House Republicans made a similar "contract" to win back the voters in the 1990's. In the contract, Trump laid out very clear, and -mostly- very real plans to put more support and more meat in his campaign. Trump promised that, "on the first day of my term of office, my administration will immediately pursue the following six measures to clean up the corruption and special interest collusion in Washington, DC" by

1. *Propose a Constitutional Amendment to impose term limits on all members of Congress;*
2. *Hiring freeze on all federal employees to reduce federal workforce through attrition (exempting military, public safety, and public health);*
3. *A requirement that for every new federal regulation, two existing regulations must be eliminated;*
4. *A 5 year-ban on White House and Congressional officials becoming lobbyists after they leave government service;*
5. *A lifetime ban on White House officials lobbying on behalf of a foreign government;*
6. *A complete ban on foreign lobbyists raising money for American elections.*

And to innovate the workforce, Donald Trump's plan is to:

1. *I will renegotiate NAFTA or withdraw from the deal under Article 2205*
2. *I will announce our withdrawal from the Trans-Pacific Partnership*
3. *I will direct my Secretary of the Treasury to label China a currency manipulator*
4. *I will direct the Secretary of Commerce and U.S. Trade Representative to identify all foreign trading abuses that unfairly impact American workers and direct them to use every tool under American and international law to end those abuses immediately*
5. *I will lift the restrictions on the production of $50 trillion dollars' worth of job-producing American energy reserves, including shale, oil, natural gas and clean coal.*
6. *Lift the Obama-Clinton roadblocks and allow vital energy infrastructure projects, like the Keystone Pipeline, to move forward*
7. *Cancel billions in payments to U.N. climate change programs and use the money to fix America's water and environmental infrastructure*

His strongest support his due to his stern, powerful, and – to some voters – aggressive security plans. He reiterates this plan here with five points:

1. *Cancel every unconstitutional executive action, memorandum and order issued by President Obama*
2. *Begin the process of selecting a replacement for Justice Scalia from one of the 20 judges on my list, who will uphold and defend the Constitution of the United States*
3. *Cancel all federal funding to Sanctuary Cities*
4. *Begin removing the more than 2 million criminal illegal immigrants from the country and cancel visas to foreign countries that won't take them back*
5. *Suspend immigration from terror-prone regions where vetting cannot safely occur. All vetting of people coming into our country will be considered extreme vetting.*

I was lazily listening to this speech, trying to take a nap actually – but I was stunned by his articulate and realistic plans Trump laid out in this speech. If he was this collected and presidential the whole campaign, he may have had my vote. With that said, his speech did include some rash and ridiculous ideas that we are all too familiar with. For one, he actually threatened to sue the women accusing him of sexual harassment. There are few people who hear of their accusations and don't have a moment to think that their testimonies are all too convenient. Secondly, Trump spat out the same brain vomit – not letting the voters forget that the system is rigged. This tantrum only makes his run for president less genuine and shows his true toddler -like character.

I think this will help his campaign recover, but with it so close to election day, a powerful gain is doubtful. Trump's Gettysburg Address just reminds the voters how close he really is to becoming president – and how passionate he has become about his movement. He promised what every American wants to hear, that he will protect "the people themselves, the great and the small, without class or difference of kind or race or origin, and undivided in interest – their freedom, their right to lift themselves from day to day and behold the things they have hoped for, and so make way for still better days for those whom they love who are to come after them." If only we didn't already know better, he could be president Trump.

October 23, 2016

If a Candidate says it – It's probably not True

You know credulity has gone too far when both candidates of an American Presidential Election are spreading conspiracy theories – and people believe them! On one side, the trailing candidate is claiming that the system is rigged, triggering a huge backlash of voters crying foul. And on the other hand, the front runner is blaming her crimes on a foreign country. The very first thing you should do – which the majority of voters do not do -is ask: What is the evidence? The Democratic candidate has been repeating repetitively that Russia has been hacking the DNC emails in a ploy to influence the 2016 elections. Part of this stems from Republican candidate Trump and Putin's seemingly close relationship, and the other part stems from Hillary's attempt to avoid being held accountable for what was inside of her emails. Among the tens of thousands of emails, there has been definitive light shed on the character of Clinton – a character that has been seen as fraudulent, vindictive, and unfair for decades. The once hero, Julian Assange has now become a Democrat nightmare as he has shifted his focus from the Bush administration to Clinton's long overdue private life. As Clinton has said, in politics, you need a private and public life – it cannot be clearer: she is corrupt.

Many people could not believe Clinton and the leading Democrats could be so rotten behind the scenes – even Barack Obama exchanged emails with Clinton's private server assuming she followed confidential protocol. The trust in Clinton was so strong that the government did conduct an investigation into the DNC email hack. Hillary has claimed that over 17 government agencies have said Russia is behind the DNC hack – like many of Clinton's automatic lies, this is probably another knee jerk lie to the public. In fact, there were only two agencies conducting investigation, the Department of National Intelligence, and the Department of Homeland Security – and they concluded that they don't have evidence that Russia is behind the hack. They clearly stated that, "...the Russians have used similar tactics and techniques across Europe and Eurasia..." but throughout the two joint investigations, they did not ever say Russia was behind the hacks. (1) So where is Hillary getting this from? Probably the same place she gets her other lies – deep within her colon.

Now, on the other side of the aisle, there has been a Trump-tantrum over the polls. They are far too close, and Trump has turned to the old "rigged poll" trick. Used in the Bush-Gore race, it is not a new strategy and it is not a strong strategy. It is so weak, very few people with a few brain cells have taken it seriously. But don't let your guard down! The lies are not the dangerous aspect of this – it is those who believe in these lies without evidence that pose a real threat to a civil election. Be mindful, credulity is everywhere – and it leave brain rot in its wake. Hopefully, we can get through this election without being overrun by gullible voters.

October 27, 2016

Do Vaccines Cause Amish Autism?

"Vaccines cause autism" – this myth is so absurd that even the most credulous don't even believe it. But that does not stop those who tend to believe despite real evidence to the contrary. In addition to this blatant lack of critical thinking, the Vaccine cause autism group has made up their own evidence to support their claim. Many groups have used fake Amish studies to prove that vaccines cause autism by stating there are no autistic Amish. If this is true, then they may have a shred of evidence to support their anti-scientific, anti-health, anti-children rhetoric. But of course it is not true.

The claim began to pick up steam when reporter, Dan Olmstead conducted a pitiful excuse for a survey in a predominantly Amish community in Pennsylvania. In the study, Olmstead foolishly claimed that out of everyone in Lancaster County, he could only find three children with autism and that two of those children were vaccinated.

A local woman told me there is one classroom with about 30 "special-needs" Amish children. In that classroom, there is one autistic Amish child. Another autistic Amish child does not go to school. The third is that woman's pre-school-age daughter. If there were more, she said, she would know it.

The most fallible part of this anti-scientific "study" is that it relies on two false assumption that the Amish do not vaccinate their children and that the Amish do not get autism. Although they are lower than the average, the Amish do actually vaccinate their children. (1) And, unfortunately, the Amish do have autism within their population anyway of a rate of 1 in 271 in a study conducted by the International Society of Autism Research. (2)

The article that spurred me to write about this myth is a recently published article by snopes – but this is a battle of wits that has been raging for a few decades now. (3) The unfortunate part of this battle of wits the vaccine – autism appears to be unarmed – how do they still seem so adamant? I think the answer lies in human nature. We have a basic need to believe things we do not understand. It is the way children learn from their parents – it is the way people communicate dangers. Like in Michael Shermer's book *Why People Believe in Weird Things*, people have a need – even an evolutionary one – to believe without investigating evidence.

Some can escape the need for evidence by fabricating their own. Just like Olmstead above, people will try to justify their credulity with fake studies and even sourcing youtube videos like fellow blogger, the "Anti-Vaccine Scientific Support Arsenal". (4) Here is an example where someone will deny evidence specifically to promote their own cause. It makes one wonder what it would take to convince these people otherwise – Can they change their mind when provided evidence, or has their brain rot infected their critical thinking faculties that much?

There shouldn't be a need for it, but extensive research has been pumped into the study of the autism-vaccine correlation. (5) At every turn, the answer is there is no relation between vaccines and autism. I would be unfair if I did not provide at least a little support for the other side, so before I post, let me mention the best way to explain the autism-vaccine correlation: http://howdovaccinescauseautism.com/

October 30, 2016

November 2016

Gullible Predictions:
Rabbi Glazerson Making Election Predictions

Christopher Hitchens once said that credulity and ignorance is a revolting characteristic in every field that has ever existed... except in religion. In the discussion of religion, you must sacrifice at least a portion of your rational faculties – the election is no different. It is difficult now a days to find a single scientific study, survey, or statistic that is not contradicted or ridiculed by some religious power. And today being Election Day, let me introduce you to some people who want to ignore even poll findings. The people of WND.com have discovered the winner of the 2016 election in the Old Testament! (1) The psychic they is is Rabbi Matityahu Glazerson – a charlatans who has sold over 30 books about using the so-called Bible code. he has even predicted the last election using the same code. (he was wrong by predicting Romney would win). (2) But this election is special – mainly because evangelicals are trying to find any reason to vote for Donald trump who is anything but a holy man. In this prediction, the Rabbi revealed this stunning coincidence:

"...published on July 6 in which Glazerson presented a Bible-code table from Deuteronomy. He pointed to the word Donald, spelled in Hebrew letters, next to the word nasi, which is Hebrew for president. He also found an abbreviation for Artzot haBrit, which is the way the United States is referred to in Hebrew..."

The prediction the Rabbi is making suggests that Donald trump is the new Cyrus the Great – a Biblical leader of Persia who let the captive Jews return back to Israel. The story hints that god used Cyrus to free the Jews back to their homeland – even though Cyrus wasn't a believer, and even though god put them in captivity anyways. Since Trump is not really a believer, we can only guess that evangelicals are using Cyrus as a way to connect him to the bible. It is a complete stretch either way. If this system worked, then why has it been wrong so far? And why isn't it used worldwide? Because it doesn't – I don't have to remind my sharp minded readers of this. But it is an important quality of irrational credulous people that others must keep in mind: they do no act within the same reality as everyone else. Besides checking in on them for a cheap laugh, we need to be reminded that this sort of non-thinking is a horrendous crime against everything our race has developed over time. So, even though now, charlatans like Rabbi Glazerson and the ones who report his "predictions" are a stain on human thought and are somewhat benign – freethinkers need to keep them in their corner and use their publications as a tool to draw some useful conclusions about their followers.

November 8, 2016

The Trump Response

Everyone has heard, but may not believe, that Donald Trump is now the president elect of the United States. He overwhelmed everyone's predictions – including mine – to earn almost 300 electoral points. He has now become the leader of the free world – and it seems everyone is going crazy.

There are riots in the streets – something that is usually a rarity after our once-peaceful presidential elections. After Obama's victories that seem ever so distant, Europeans were shocked that there was not more tension. The United States have become known as the Land of the Free – especially after transitions of power. This is not the case anymore. There are fires in the streets, the Canadian immigration website has crashed from traffic, and the Trump HQ had to be surrounded by sandbags to protect from attacks. Does this seem reasonable?

The most outrage is not in the streets of Berkeley, L.A. and Pittsburgh – but online! The keyboard warriors of the millennial class are hard on the attack. And though their concerns are not for naught, but the offensive against Trump is absolutely a knee jerk reaction that reeks of illogical and blind anger.

Ellie Weissel is spinning in his grave and thousands of Tumblrs are claiming "now we know what the Jews felt like". Disgruntled youths have started the #notmypresident tag. What an absolutely ridiculous idea! The fact that they think their opinions trumps democracy (pun intended). The overwhelming amount of violent tempered brain rot is littering the internet and it does not stop at Facebook and Twitter. Though liberal, the occasionally moderate sites like The Atlantic and The Slate have been on an outright rampage – and definitely not helping the fury of the protesters.

The hero of this situation has come from the most unlikely place: the oval office. That's right: Mr Obama has come out of this mess as a level-headed leader in preserving democracy and ensuring a smooth transition of power. Even though Obama has campaigned for ally Clinton, his unnerving wit and articulate, rational commitment to the office has shown through. If the protesters had a shred of Obama's honor, there would be no problem with this transition. President Obama is even inviting trump to the White house on Thursday to share his plan for a peaceful transition of power – a plan that has been in the works for a year. In his speech, Obama caught my attention almost immediately:

Now, it is no secret that the president-elect and I have some pretty significant differences. But remember, eight years ago President Bush and I had some pretty significant differences. But President Bush's team could not have been more professional or more gracious in making sure we had a smooth transition so that we could hit the ground running.

I did not vote for Obama in either the 2008 or 2012 election – but I am extremely glad he won. He broke my automatic pull towards Republicans and opened my mind to Democrats by leading a strong, composed, and uplifting 2 terms. Obama will be known for the first black president second, and a cool headed leader first. Let me end with the part of his speech everyone needs to hear:

Now, everybody is sad when their side loses an election, but the day after we have to remember that we're actually all on one team. This is an intramural scrimmage. We're not Democrats first. We're not Republicans first. We are Americans first. We're patriots first.

We all want what's best for this country. That's what I heard in Mr. Trump's remarks last night. That's what I heard when I spoke to him directly. And I was heartened by that. That's what the country needs — a sense of unity, a sense of inclusion, a respect for our institutions, our way of life, rule of law, and respect for each other.

I hope that he maintains that spirit throughout this transition. And I certainly hope that's how his presidency has a chance to begin.

November 10, 2016

Panic, uncertainty, fear, and anger is flooding the streets across America since the President elect Donald Trump won the 2016 election. This clearly primal and barbaric response has truly brought out the worst in young Democrats. But nothing is as shameful and deplorable than what happened just hours after Trump was elected president.

In Baton Rouge Louisiana, a report came in that a young Muslim woman was assaulted on the campus of Lafayette University. (1) Reportedly, the 18 year old woman claims that two white men wearing white Trump hats yelled racial slurs, then attacked her with a metal pipe, and stole her purse and Hijab. The same day, police at San Diego University reported another attack in which a Muslim student was harassed with offensive slurs about her faith and her car keys and car was stolen. The following morning, yet another Muslim woman was attacked. Two white men drove up to her in a sedan and struck her with a metal object and stole her wallet and Hijab – all while yelling obscenities at her.

In every case, these women declined medical treatment, even though one was reported to have been "knocked out". And unless, the men can travel from Baton Rouge to San Diego and back to Baton Rouge, these reports seem false. Like many of the other shamefully disgusting, this seems to be an attempt at validating all the unreasonable violence being spurred on by the #notmypresident gang.

And these false allegations are not the first ones. Many popular myths have been spread by the all powerful Tumblr and Facebook with as little proof as possible. A recent myth is that Trump supporters chanted "We hate Muslims, we hate Blacks, we want our great country back" during a rally. This is of course proven false by the people at snopes.com (2)

And it must be said that there is legitimate attacks out there and the scum who commit these crimes deserve the fullest extent of the law. Such as in the case where University of Wisconsin-Stout, Hussain Saeed Alnahdi was attacked and later died from his wounds at the hospital. (3) Mr. Alnahdi did not deny medical assistance – this was a real attack on him. The false claims of attack and bigotry are shameful at best and shallow and divisive at its worst. There is no doubt more false reports will follow mirroring the rape allegations that arise periodically. Similarly, these two are out of frustration and is simply a pitiful call for action.

November 11, 2016

The Thomas Jefferson Series

The stereotypical god-like praise for the Founding Father's receive are pounded into the American children beginning in grade school. It is not uncommon to develop a nihilist point of view towards these sage historical figures. But when one matures and learns about the issue of individual freedom and how our country's ideals came to be, the Founding Fathers become a central icon for liberty. In my opinion, there is no grater hero than the Sage of Monticello himself: Thomas Jefferson. Most know him from the lowly nickel, but Jefferson, our third president has done far more for establishing the theme of personal freedom, fighting against the forces who threaten our liberties, and most importantly, built up the wall that stands today between the Church and State. As Christopher Hitchens coined:

"Mr. Jefferson; build up that wall!"

Because of his importance, I will be doing a short series on him throughout the month to go over his accomplishments and legacy. My more pessimistic readers will already have a list in their head about all the scandals and myths regarding Mr. Jefferson. Rest assured, I will also try to cover the more popular stories about the president to debunk any false ones.

November 18, 2016

Jeffersonian Hate

As with nearly every single historical figure, American Founding Father, Thomas Jefferson possesses his fair share of misinformation, brain rot, and defaming untruths. Recently, the University of Virginia president, Teresa Sullivan, quoted Thomas Jefferson during a speech on campus and a petition of over 469 signatures was created in response. (1) Thomas Jefferson, the founder of the University of Virginia, held that as one of his biggest accomplishment in his epitaph – listing it above being president, "Author of the Declaration of Independence [and] of the Statute of Virginia for religious freedom & Father of the University of Virginia." But in today's society, not even the most secular, freedom loving, slavery hating Founding Father is safe from criticism.

Assistant Professor of Psychology, Noelle Hurd, who started the petition tried to defend her actions, "I think that Jefferson is often celebrated for his accomplishments with little or no acknowledgement of the atrocities he committed against hundreds of human beings" The atrocities mentioned was the ownership of slaves. Anyone with a high school education would know that Jefferson was a stanch opponent of slavery calling it a "moral depravity" and a "hideous blot". Slavery stood against everything Jefferson held dear, including the all-important idea of personal liberty – of which slavery is unnatural. (2) In 1778, Jefferson wrote a law to prohibit importing African slaves. Again, in 1784, he tried to pass an ordinance that would ban slavery in Northwest Territories.

Many opponents of Jefferson even try to use Jefferson's own words against him. In an article in the Atlantic, Conor Cruise O'Brien – through his drivel – tried to pin the terms "Radical and Racist" to Mr. Jefferson. O'Brien really had to reach far by using the quote used in the Jefferson Memorial to tag him as a racist. (3) The quote is as follows:
Indeed I tremble for my country when I reflect that God is just, that his justice cannot sleep forever. Commerce between master and slave is despotism. Nothing is more certainly written in the book of fate than that these people are to be free.

O'Brien continues the quote to include the rest of Jefferson's sentence, "Nor is it less certain that the two races, equally free, cannot live in the same government. Nature, habit, opinion has drawn indelible lines of distinction between them." Now, a rational adult would take this as it was meant: to say that if the two races were made equal, by abolishing slavery, there would be incredible tension between the two. Which of course there was tension. From the Emancipation Proclamation to even today, there has been ugly discrimination which most people today wouldn't dare to defy.

What O'Brien claims this quote means is, "In short, these people are to be free, and then deported. Jefferson's teaching on that matter is quite clear". If anyone needs a definition of "Brain Rot" here we have it. This article was published in the early 90's, and no doubt Mr. O'Brien cringes in regret – for no amount of untruth has been published in The Atlantic since. But the stigma lives on – and lives on Virginia University no less.

If we as a nation truly desire secular tolerance in America, we need to stop the friendly fire. Thomas Jefferson is centuries ahead of his time, and with writers like Conor O'Brien, Jefferson seems ahead of our time as well.

November 15, 2016

The Religion of Thomas Jefferson

The Founding Fathers are tirelessly put in a heroic and religious light. Schools and organizations with a more holy influence try to fit these morally superior men into their own spheres of thought, or lack thereof – but the Founding Fathers were far from religious. They were agnostic at most – but none were more skeptical, and thoughtful than Thomas Jefferson who, in his work, has done strenuous work to free people from the clutch of the church.

Having had recently suffered from the First Great Awakening in the mid 1700's the British colonies saw a major move to the church – more specifically, the Anglican Church. Seeing the chance for regional power that was impossible in Europe, the Anglican Church took the opportunity for power. In Thomas Jefferson's beloved state of Virginia, the church took extreme actions to secure their hold on the land. In short, the state and the religion became intertwined. Public officials in Virginia must swear to the 39 articles of the Anglican church; the general assembly of Virginia made it a crime to violate church doctrine; the 1705 statute required anyone who held office to believe in the Christian church in order to, "hold and enjoy any office or employment, ecclesiastical, civil, or military".

At the time, more loose doctrine started to challenge and take away from the Anglican Church. Churches such as the Baptist and Presbyterian started to take members away from the Anglican hold – sparking more authoritarian action from the ruling religion. Anyone who was not a member of their specific church was labeled "dissenters" – mainly those who were a part of the new realism movement. In response, all ministers must be licensed and registered with the church. If not, they would be considered "street preachers" and were jailed for heresy. This cannot go on in any healthy society, but certainly not in Jefferson's homestead.

IN PUBLIC LIFE
Thomas Jefferson, a liberty-loving open-minded man, seems to have never been very religious. And from the very beginning of the creation of the new Union, he had been hard at work to make America a secular, freedom loving nation. There is, of course, the freedom to exercise religion clause in the Declaration of Rights – but Jefferson originally submitted a draft for a more bold stance in religion:

> *"All persons shall have full and free liberty of religious opinion; nor shall any be compelled to frequent or maintain any religious institution"*

This was struck down by the general assembly – but Jefferson's work did not stop there. When the new Virginia General Assembly met, Jefferson's first purposeful was to repeal the tax funding of the Anglican Church. Seeing as less than half of all Virginians were Anglican, the tax funding was an insult and an infringement on the rights of his fellow Virginians. The result was that all "dissenters" were exempt from paying any tax to the church – thus the beginning of the end of the Churches hold.

The next step was Jefferson's prized Act to Establish Religious Freedom. To win support, Jefferson reasoned that "the Almighty God hath created the mind free" so that the "religious opinions and beliefs" must also remain free. Just like that, Jefferson freed the nation as well as the mind of compulsory church devotion. This accomplishment is listed in his epitaph along with his authorship of the Declaration of Independence as well as his founding of the Virginia University who has recently disappointed their founder by banishing any quotes from him. Notice the three accomplishments he wanted to be remembered for and you will see that his leadership in the revolutions in America and France; leadership in the Barbary Wars; and being the 3rd President of the United States was not mentioned. Instead, his voice of reason through the Declaration of Independence, religious freedoms, and his founding of the University is his shining pride.

"HERE WAS BURIED

THOMAS JEFFERSON

AUTHOR OF THE DECLARATION

OF

AMERICAN INDEPENDENCE

OF THE

STATUE OF VIRGINIA

FOR

RELIGIOUS FREEDOM

AND THE FATHER OF THE

UNIVERSITY OF VIRGINIA

IN PERSONAL LIFE

It was in Jefferson's more personal works that we see his real feelings toward religion. Mr. Jefferson even created his own version of the New Testament by taking a knife to it – cutting out anything that is fantastic, or wicked, or mythical, or silly – creating an extremely shorter version. In his view, Christianity was a silly concept of which defiles reason. Any action in the direction of reason was a good one in his eyes:

"No one sees with greater pleasure than myself the progress of reason in it's advances towards rational Christianity. when we shall have done away the incomprehensible jargon of the Trinitarian arithmetic, that three are one, and one is three; when we shall have knocked down the artificial scaffolding, reared to mask from view the simple structure of Jesus, when, in short, we shall have unlearned every thing which has been taught since his day, and got back to the pure and simple doctrines he inculcated, we shall then be truly and worthily his disciples: and my opinion is that if nothing had ever been added to what flowed purely from his lips, the whole world would at this day have been Christian. I know that the case you cite, of Dr Drake, has

been a common one. the religion-builders have so distorted and deformed the doctrines of Jesus, so muffled them in mysticisms, fancies and falsehoods, have caricatured them into forms so monstrous and inconceivable, as to shock reasonable thinkers, to revolt them against the whole, and drive them rashly to pronounce its founder an imposter..."

Many people believe that the founding fathers were agnostic at best, but some like Richard Dawkins and Christopher Hitchens think that if certain scientific discoveries were around at the time of the fathers, then they would definitely be atheists. This idea pronounces itself in the discussion of slavery – and on the very Jefferson Memorial itself, he is quoted saying, *"Indeed I tremble for my country when I reflect that God is just, that his justice cannot sleep forever. Commerce between master and slave is despotism. Nothing is more certainly written in the book of fate than that these people are to be free. Establish a law for educating the common people. This it is the business of the state and on a general plan."*

Many Americans today would be shocked to hear the Founding Father speaking so. Jefferson, himself, would be shocked to know about certain traditions we have today such as National Day of Prayers, including god in our currency, and god in the pledge of allegiance. What is even more surprising is how comfortable Congress was with secularism at Jefferson's time. At the end of the Barbary Wars, Jefferson and his Congress wrote and unanimously passed the Peace Treaty stating that *"the Government of the United States of America is not, in any sense, founded on the Christian religion"*

Rather than turn away from the our Founding Fathers, I would hope respect is kept for them, remembering that they were centuries ahead of their time – the only men capable to fully and successfully create such an amazing Union. Thomas Jefferson, above the rest, stood for reason and thought, especially in the face of religious supremacy. Who today have the balls to stand up against irrational beliefs so fervently? Using Jefferson's own words, I beg that everyone could find it in them to, *"question with boldness even the existence of a god; because if there be one he must approve of the homage of reason more than that of blindfolded fear"*

November 21, 2016

Thomas Jefferson on Slavery

It is of no exaggeration to say that Thomas Jefferson, or any of the Founding Fathers, were far ahead of their time. But when it comes to the rather repulsive issue of slavery, Thomas Jefferson is at least 100 years ahead of his time. Having had seen so many uneducated claims that Jefferson was a racist and a bigot on social media, news articles, and more recently within the University of Virginia: the very University Jefferson founded, I have been called to action to try and clear some of the myths – the biggest myth being his stance on slavery.

The author of the Declaration of Independence, and the one who coined the term that "all men are created equal", Thomas Jefferson is known as the sage of Monticello, and the Sage of liberty. Having said that, it is difficult for me to wrap my head around the fact that such negative and slanderous rumors have boiled out of the uneducated masses of the young left. And yet, here we are: at a point in history where we must defend an anti-slavery, pro-liberty Founding Father of America. Assistant Professor of Psychology, Noelle Hurd, who started a petition against using Jefferson in quotes on the Virginia University campus has claimed, "I think that Jefferson is often celebrated for his accomplishments with little or no acknowledgement of the atrocities he committed against hundreds of human beings" (1)

Let's unpack this claim – Jefferson must be spinning around in his grave at this point. "the atrocities he committed against hundreds of human beings" – I cannot think of any atrocities committed besides Jefferson and the slaves. before we go into that, it is important to first look at his words and actions in regards to slavery. (2) It is a well-known and documented fact that Jefferson was completely anti-slavery stating it is a "moral depravity" as well as a "hideous blot" on mankind's history. Furthermore, he believed that slavery posed the greatest threat to the survival of America as a nation due to its divisiveness and suppression of life and liberty. When the Founding Fathers began the legislation to start the new nation, Jefferson was adamant about including the abolition of slavery. (3) In his home state of Virginia in 1778 – a hundred years before Lincoln's time – Jefferson drafted a law that would prohibit the importation of enslaved Africans. Just 6 years later, Jefferson came back to propose an ordinance to ban slavery in the Northwest Territories (Ohio, Indiana, Illinois, Michigan area). Arguably, having these territories set the North up for an anti-slavery stance during the pre-Civil War tensions. In the Jefferson Memorial itself, a quote by Jefferson states that, "I tremble for my country to think that god is just, that his justice cannot sleep forever" – noting the deplorable slavery of hundreds of thousands of people in Virginia alone.

The failure of the majority of his propositions has mainly been attributed to the reality of slavery already so depended on and entrenched in the economy and culture of the young nation. When Jefferson was born, slavery had already existed to far too long – nearly 75 years! He grew up around it and luckily rejected the depravity. At the point of death, the slave population in Virginia had reached almost 450,000. Jefferson had hopped that the North's abolition of slavery would, in time, lead to the overall elimination of slavery – and of course he was wrong. He did take an incredibly brave stance against slavery that ultimately lead to the anti-slavery North and arguably influenced Lincoln's point of view as well – in a letter from 1859, Lincoln explains his thoughts on Jefferson's ideals, saying (4):

All honor to Jefferson – to the man who, in the concrete pressure of a struggle for national independence by a single people, had the coolness, forecast, and capacity to introduce into a merely revolutionary document, an abstract truth, applicable to all men and all times, and so embalm it there, that to-day, and in all coming days, it shall be a rebuke and a stumbling-block to the very harbingers of re-appearing tyranny and oppression.

Anyone, including the uninformed masses at the University of Virginia, claiming Jefferson was a force for evil clearly have no idea what they are talking about. It wouldn't surprise me one bit if these people's brains have succumbed to rot so far to their core that they would claim Lincoln was pro-slavery. It does exist.

The last point that must be made is one that is probably at the center of the anti-Jeffersonian rhetoric – that is the fact that Jefferson owned slaves. A lesser known fact, but Jefferson had bondsman on his property of Monticello. In the book Author of America, it i mentioned that Jefferson received the slaves from his father in-law and begrudgingly kept some of them. In time he did free seven of the members of the Hemmings family – the family I will talk about in a later post. The slaves he did keep were known to have been treated exceptionally well. One problem with freeing large groups of slaves is that they ran the risk of being captured and re-enslaved to a worse matter than before. Because of that, freeing all of his slaves was just not practical or ideal for the bondsman. Jefferson was a lover of freedom and loved his slaves like his own family – there is still a small graveyard at Monticello where Mr. Jefferson buried his slaves. A practice that is largely unheard of. Like I said, I will go into the Hemings relationship with Jefferson in a later post, but let me leave this one with a quote that perfectly embodies Jefferson's feelings about slavery from a letter to Thomas Cooper in 1814 (5):

There is nothing I would not sacrifice to a practicable plan of abolishing every vestige of this moral and political depravity.

November 23, 2016

Thomas Jefferson's Scandal

Perhaps one of the biggest human flaw is accepting truths before researching the facts. This is the case for far too many issues today, but everyone falls victim to this flaw at least once – I, victim to this human error more than I can count. The scandal regarding Thomas Jefferson and his slaves is one that I have not truly researched and accepted for fact until now.

The rumors from the 1700's to DNA tests in the 1990's have damned Jefferson's reputation and deemed him a rapist. If, indeed, Jefferson did have a relationship with his slaves, it may only help his anti-slavery stance. But the damning part about the scandal is that he was labeled a rapist. This fact the the author of the Declaration of Independence was a rapist could stain his freedom-loving reputation with hypocrisy and racism. Thankfully, for those who revere Jefferson as a man of morality and liberty, it is not true.

The story that originally got so much attention was the DNA test that claimed Thomas Jefferson was the father of at least 2 of Sally Hemings children. The reason for the immediate attention is simply because we love a good scandal. The drama of our past still lives through a Lifetime Network-like need for drama. The very first studies that caught the public eye is the 1953 study by Fawn Brodie that seemed to have hinted at the Heming relationship. (1) From there the rumors spread to more publications by historian Henry Randall who claimed, *"She [Hemings] had children which resembled Mr. Jefferson so closely that it was plain that they had his blood in their veins ... He [Randolph] said in one instance, a gentleman dining with Mr. Jefferson, looked so startled as he raised his eyes from the latter to the servant behind him, that his discovery of the resemblance was perfectly obvious to all."* (2)

These hearsay claims are not without legitimate studies to accompany it. The 1998 DNA study sealed Mr. Jefferson's fate by claiming with 100% certainty that Sally Heming's son, Eston was his child. (3) This study is based on the Y-chromosome of the sons of Miss Hemings to link the males together. The only problem is that Jefferson's DNA was not used and he did not have any descendants to use for DNA. There have been many protests to the study due to it's faulty science. Dr. Eugene Foster investigated the claims and found that it is extremely unlikely to have any DNA link between Heming's children and Mr. Jefferson. (4) In fact, there is overwhelming evidence to the contrary. In a collaborative study, PBS published the evidence attempting to debunk the bogus studies of the past (5) :

1. Tested Subjects

Thomas Jefferson had no male descendants to test so a direct link to Sally Hemings children could not be tested. To run the DNA test, Eugene Foster used material from male relatives to Jefferson. So the results leave 8 possible father's if the results are positive...and the results gives a <1% probability.

2. Rare Halotype

The average frequency of a genetic halotype like Jefferson's is about 1.5%. It has never been observed outside the Jefferson family, and it was not found among a sample of 670 European or 1,200 people worldwide – and not found in Heming's children

3. Nonspecific DNA results

In Dr. Foster's results, he found that the 1% match was with Eston Hemings and the descendants of Thomas Jefferson's Uncle, Field Jefferson. This leads us to the next problem with the results

4. Multiple Possible links

The DNA tests indicated that any one of 8 Jeffersons could have been the father of Eston with a 1% certainty and there was nothing to indicate it was Thomas. The 8 possibilities identified by the DNA tests are Thomas, Randolph (Jefferson's brother), Randolph's 5 sons, and a cousin George and in 5 of Randolph's sons, who were in their teens or 20's when Sally Hemings was having children.

5. Misleading results

Again, the most damning part of the case against Jefferson is the drama oriented media. The media reacts to good juicy stories like the public does: it accepts it as fact if they want it to be a fact. After the DNA test came out, CNN reported the study with the headline "Jefferson Fathered Slave's Last Child".

6. New Results

In March of 2000, new DNA results came from the Woodson Association to show that "beyond any reasonable doubt that Thomas Jefferson was not the father". The only reason the results did not get as much attention is because it did not conform to the more Jerry Springer-like results.

7. Grave located

Those who desire a Heming-Jeffersonian link keep claiming they know where William Hemings grave is. William Hemings, the missing link the Heming family is basing their relationship on. But the true grave has finally been found and negates any facts relying on the original grave site and puts any other facts relying on oral history in a skeptical light.

8. Thomas Jefferson Exhumation

If Thomas Jefferson were exhumed for Y chromosome DNA testing it would only confirm that he carried the same Y chromosome as the other 7 Jeffersons in question. The only way this would not be true is if Thomas Jefferson were illegitimate. Besides being futile, it is very unlikely that there would be usable DNA that could be tested after so many years.

9. Illegitimacy

The genetic trail also could have been broken in subsequent generations if any of the mothers in the presumed chain actually had her son by a man outside the Jefferson line. Some of the Hemings' lines cannot be tested, as there are no male line descendants.

In short, this scandal has gone on for far too long and has even tarnished Jefferson's reputation to such an extent that he is labelled a racist and bigot by the Black Lives Matters organization. (6) If only there are more fact checkers to spread the word. The lesson to this: questions everything, because ignorance is a strong weapon. So strong, it has blemished the strongest warrior of freedom. That should be enough to disturb anyone who values facts and skepticism.

November 28, 2016

Thomas Paine: The Original Emancipator

"There's no real memorial to him in his country of birth. There's no day that honors him. He's not taught in schools. There's no real memorial to him in his country of adoption tough he is really the unofficial founding father and, undoubtedly, the moral author of the Declaration of Independence" - Triumvirate of Rationalism

Thomas Paine is an incredibly illusive figure in history, and yet he was the emancipator of thought, philosophy, and liberty. Very little is known about him save that he was a corset maker until he took up the sexier career of a political writer - and in the process made history. His two bestselling pamphlets Common Sense and the Rights of Man brought revolution out of the hands of Monarchs and Priests and into the hands and minds of the common man. It was in those conveniently short pamphlets that Paine was able to gather support for the American and French Revolutions - and ultimately, across the world. The idea that rights belong to every man was a rare ideal. At the time, there was an iron grip on rights by the Kings and a monopoly on morality by the Church. It was a common insult to Democracy to equate it to the "mob rule" or a barbarian frenzy. But Paine brought it to everyone. Rights come from a time before Priests and Kings - they are inherent and innate.

In France, Paine correctly pointed out that feudalism is over now - it wasn't just the king or this queen that was overthrown, but rather the hereditary principle in France that has been destroyed. These "predatory governments" can only be beaten by the fellow man - because it is only in the hearts of the patriot that rights can truly be asserted. Even in the 1700's, philosophy was reserved for the elite to be revered by the poor - so there were very few thought provoking philosophers available for the common man. The two that were, continually butting heads. John Locke and Thomas Hobbes argued about whether here were rights and where they came from, how they came to be and to whom they applied. This discussion, though known, was something of a private discussion. Paine smashed that private discussion and made it available to all. It was the other way a true grassroots movement could be formed - And it resulted in the two greatest revolutions in history.

Simply put, the concept of rights was monopolized by the theologians and church philosophers. It was the Catholic Church who fought any sort of knowledge spreading by banning translations of the Bible and even killed heretics for interpenetration it incorrectly. One thinks of Blaise Pascal' wager against thought, "God is or He is not. But to which side shall we incline? Reason can decide on nothing here." Not only does reason have no bearing to religion and thought, but you should simply believe in god because the punishment is so severe, you might as well believe (as if it is that easy to do). Any suspension of reason is pure brain rot – and the common man's place in the argument void. It was Thomas Paine who, so appropriately stated, "The world is my country, my mind is my church, and my religion is to do good". This was the end goal of the revolution – and what a milestone! Thomas Paine is truly the original emancipator of man.

November 29, 2016

Fidel Castro Defended

There has been no better end to the long list of high-profile deaths in 2016 than the death of the infamous dictator: Fidel Castro. Dying at the age of 90, Castro has committed an innumerable amount of atrocities throughout his rein on the communist island – but many have forgotten this. Even worse – they applaud it! One would think that centuries of having to watch on as political enemies are killed or worse, we could at least recognize Castro for what he was: a brutal homicidal dictator. In case we need reminding, I will list his worst crimes and follow it up with those who mourn this monster's death.

It is well known that within the Cuban Communist Revolution – and every Communist Revolution – there were thousands murdered for the sake of the revolution. The more well-known mass murderers like Stalin, Pol Pat, and Hitler killed more in number, but the ratio of body count to Cuban population is devastating. British historian Hugh Thomas estimates at least 5,000 executions before 1970 – 2,113 of them being public executions. Other researchers believe even more were killed after 1970. Political professor at the University of Hawaii, Rudolph J. Rummel estimated about 15,000 deaths from 1958 – 1980. (1) The lucky victims of his bloody thirsty aggression were deported or fled to Florida where they are still celebrating his death to this day. That was his biggest crime, but because some seem to think a few thousands dead is forgivable, let me list out some of the details of his purging. We cannot forget that he did try and stop the families of political enemies as they fled the island. He even sank the tugboat "13 de Marzo" and killed the women and children aboard. (2) If anyone is horrified at the images of the Syrian refugees dying in their trek to Europe, then please remember: this was right off the coast of Florida. In addition to murder, Fidel also has another shocking similarity to Hitler and Stalin: Concentration Camps. The Castro regime called them "Military Units to Aid Production" or UMAPs. (3) They were forced agricultural labor camps used to imprison the families of suspected political crimes. If that isn't enough to condemn this man, maybe his crimes against the gay community will. (4) About 10% of inmates in the camps were homosexual men that he regarded as "antisocial" or "counter revolutionary". (5) In 1967, a human rights organization, the "Organization of American States" reported that over 30,000 inmates were "forced to work for free in state farms from 10 to 12 hours a day, from sunrise to sunset, seven days per week, poor alimentation with rice and spoiled food, unhealthy water, unclean plates, congested barracks, no electricity, latrines, no showers, inmates are given the same treatment as political prisoners." (6) The atrocities are so bad even the deplorable dictator himself admitted in an interview that "yes, there were moments of great injustice, great injustice!" Can you imagine a more greasy pitiful worm of a man?

If one can imagine, in the year 2016, these war crimes are being overlooked. Let me being a short list of those who forgotten the thousands who have died at Castro's hands or actually praised him.

President Barack Obama did not mention any crimes and merely said, "History will record and judge the enormous impact of this singular figure on the people and world around him"

Fidel Castro had received three Popes throughout his life time: Pope Benedict XVI, Pope John Paul II, and Pope Francis. None of them condemning the crimes committed to his own people – many of them members of the Catholic church! Maybe god had a special plan for them? here is what Pope Francis had to say about Castro:

"Upon receiving the sad news of the death of your dear brother, His Excellency Mister Fidel Alejandro Castro Ruz, former president of the State Council and of the Government of the Republic of Cuba, I express my sentiments of sorrow to Your Excellency and other family members of the deceased dignitary, as well as to the people of this beloved nation"

Green Party Presidential candidate speaks volumes about her own values by tweeting "Fidel Castro was a symbol of the struggle for justice in the shadow of empire. Presente!"

Surprisingly, Clinton recently called out Sanders regarding his past praise of Fidel's Cuba when he said, "revolution of values' in Cuba, and talked about how people were working for the common good, not for themselves". The shameful praise was defended by Sanders, but the fact that he defended a murderer and called out by a liar, stains his idea of freedom.

Other politicians who gave condolences to the Cuban Dictator include, but are not limited to: Canadian Prime Minister Justin Trudeau, former U.S. President Jimmy Carter, the United Kingdom's Labor Party leader Jeremy Corbyn, Irish President Michael Higgins, and Iranian Supreme Leader Ayatollah Khamenei.

Fidel Castro must join the growing list of the anti democratic dictators throughout history if we wish to keep a stern and noble expectation of freedom in the future. How can we set an example for Democracy while praising dictators? How can the catholic Church claim to be representing god while praising those who kill his children? If you are a fan of Liberty, we need to come together in unison to draw a line in the sand. This will keep democracy healthy, and our conscience clean.

November 30, 2016

December 2016

The Jedi Legacy

The Daily Skeptic Blog has been far from "daily" as of late – the main reason is that I started a new job and had my first baby. While I settle into the new life as a proud daddy, please bear with me as I post non-news essays about various topics.

In case you haven't notice, the Skeptic Blog has been leaning more and more toward personal liberty and individualist-type as those characteristics are necessary to achieve a skeptical mind-set. Here is an essay I wrote for fun back in January in 2016 about the Jedi morals from the Star Wars saga. Having have been a big Star Wars fan (movies and the now obsolete extended universe, of course), I kept finding deep anti-democratic, anti-liberty, anti-individualist sentiment within the Jedi order – I saw this attitude so often within the original, prequel, and books, it seems almost like a theme for the Jedi. When one sees the immoral, irrational Jedi within this light, I think it brings more rationality to Anakin's fall away from the Order and more beauty to Luke's own reformation to the Order. Enjoy my early writing, I will be posting more of these.

It is not long after one begins the Star Wars trilogy, either in the films or the books, does one face the dark side of the force, the dreaded Sith Lords. Consistently the antagonists throughout the epic story, the Siths are users of the force just like the Jedi and yet the Siths are seen as being 'the bad guys' always hidden in the shadows in defiance against the Jedi's fight for peace and justice in the galaxy. Because it is easy to label the Jedi as the heroes they appear to be, I run the obvious risk of sounding like a crazy contrarian seeking to critique any aspect of popular opinion. That maybe the case, but I aim to dissect the Jedi order in comparison to the Sith order to reveal that even the Jedi and Sith cannot be taken at face value. Bear with me as I daringly seek to shine new light on the Dark Side of the force.

As any novice Star Wars fan knows, there is the Force controlling and guiding every living thing in the universe, "it's an energy field created by all living things. It surrounds us and penetrates us; it binds the galaxy together" as Obi Wan so poetically puts it in Star Wars: A New Hope. Throughout the galaxy there are some who possess the ability to control and manipulate the Force, and based on the individual's character, intentions, and emotions they use either the light side or the dark side of the force. Almost immediately, as if run by a totalitarian censorship, the two sides of control is painted as good and bad – please remain skeptical of this assumption (but if you don't, I will do that work for you). The light side of the force is how the Jedi are supposed to use it and is routinely characterized as being compassionate, mindful, and just. The dark side of the force however, is reserved for passion, hate, and fear; characteristics we associate with evil actions but – may I remind the reader – these characteristics are all too human. They are built within us and are a part of any emotional human being.

I must digress. The Jedi have helped the galaxy keep peace for over 50,000 years by using these powers. It isn't until a rogue Jedi, leaving the order to collect followers and colonizes natives of Korriban, who from the inhabitants name sake, they coin the phrase "Sith". These Force manipulators, with an imbedded hatred for the Jedi, spark many wars and because of their short lived passion, lacks of numbers, and lack of unity, are beaten by the Jedi. The main actors in these first encounters with the Jedi order are not important up until 1,000 B.B.Y. as far as the Sith philosophy goes. I am putting myself in an uncomfortable firing zone with the Sith lore fans, so I must clarify: these Sith Lords, between the time they left the Jedi and until 1000 years before A New Hope, are interesting in their own respects while they pave the way for the most recent Siths and they deserve investigation from those truly interested in them. But, for the sake of reviewing the core Sith philosophy, they can be ignored for now.

In the movies, there is a prophesy continuously, yet vaguely, brought up by the Jedi that someone from their ranks are supposed to rise up and bring balance to the force; the character in question in Anakin Skywalker who, after becoming frustrated with the Jedi Order, is lead to the dark side where he assists Darth Plagues in exterminating the Jedi. An unimaginable and dramatic feat leads the Jedi survivors to believe Anakin was not the person in the prophecy. Just as Greek mythology is based on assumptions and misunderstandings, so is the Jedi interpretation of their fate. It is released to the audience in Return of the Jedi, that Anakin really is the one who balances the force by killing Darth Plagues. A point that seems to be missed is that Anakin whipped out the Jedi and the Sith parties. The importance of the actions of Anakin is not just to purge the Jedi (which the audience sees as a great tragedy), but to destroy both parties from the galaxy and thus balancing the force. The Force, constantly and unbiasly guiding the universe, could not have balanced itself out without first purging the Jedi in genocide; which leads to my main argument: the Jedi were tainted by backwards hypocritical dogma in which a balanced force could not be realized.

Little known to the moviegoers, the Sith also have their own prophesy that is much more honest and brutal than the Jedi one. The prophecy says that there will be a Sith (titled Sith'ari), who will be so strong they will purge the ranks of the Sith and through the strongest will continue to rule the galaxy. Again, this prophecy is sometimes misinterpreted as being false. But young Darth Bane, rising through the Sith Academy in a Jedi-Sith war 1,000 B.B.Y., destroys the Sith Lords in battle and begins his reign with the Rule of Two which sets the rule for the Siths from then on: only two Sith could exist at any given time. A Dark Lord of the Sith to embody power, and an apprentice to crave it. For the next 1,000 years, the Siths remained in hiding following this rule while also gaining power, money, and knowledge all without the attention of the aloof Jedi.

The successful completion of the Sith prophecy is needed in order for the completion of the Jedi prophecy. Both – and I mean both – factions must be eliminated to balance the galaxy. Some may ask why the Jedi needed to be purged, and I am glad they asked. The Jedi, even when compared to the Sith are a force for evil in that galaxy while hiding behind an ever distorted mask of morality and justice. To continue, a comparison must be made between the two parties philosophy. Luckily, we have been given two "codes" for the Sith and Jedi. The Jedi Code is as follows:

There is no emotion, there is peace

There is no ignorance, there is knowledge

There is no passion, there is serenity

There is no chaos, there is harmony

There is no death, there is the Force

The common Star Wars fan should have no problem with this code as it reflects exactly what is intended. Meek and mild Jedi: out to save the day in a peaceful and mindful way. The skeptic of readers should be able to pick out one or two contradictions in this code as well as in the Jedi actions including but absolutely not limited to the restriction of knowledge, eager war mongering, and child abduction to name a few. Before I get started ranting about the Jedi order and risk losing myself, let me now present the Sith code:

Peace is a lie, there is only passion.

Through passion, I gain strength.

Through strength, I gain power.

Through power, I gain victory.

Through victory, my chains are broken.

The Force shall free me.

The Sith code, being modeled purposely after the Jedi code, states more clearly that the Sith realize that the human passion guides everything. This passion, whether it be hatred, fear, love, or even happiness will bring about strength to obtain the power that is their victory. My first argument in defense of the Sith is that they are human. They realize that they must use their unrelenting human emotions that are undeniably apart of everyone in every way the Jedi code is not.

As the code suggests, the Jedi are supposed to be protectors of peace and justice throughout the galaxy and just like the guards in Plato's The Republic are supposed to be humble protectors of the Republic, the Jefi are to be examples of morality. It is this sense of morality the jedi use to cling to the ledge of power within the galaxy. The Galactic Republic seems to be able to hold their own against the various wars and yet the Jedi are always there ready to attack. Wars such as the Mandalorian wars, in which the Jedi provoked and slaughter the Mandalorian race, and in the Clone Wars the Jedi's were all too ready to abandon their sense of peace to send their Jedi into battle. If the Jedi were as peaceful as their code suggests, they may have given into some debate as to if they should involve themselves. Maybe the authoritarian Jedi Counsel may have attempted more diplomacy before the genocide they have committed.

Almost just as war hungry, Yoda and Mace Windu, in their Clone Wars, show that the Order has not changed and will not change when their power is threatened. Instead, they have undemocratically sealed their fate by throwing all Jedi into the fray forcing their fighters (and child soldiers) to fight in a war that does not involve them. If more democracy was used to make decisions, there would be no doubt to think Anakin would have sided with the Jedi. The same hypocritical peacefulness can be seen throughout history with figures like Gandhi and Muhammad who seem peaceful, lead their numbers to death for their own selfish cause.

Another crime with which the Jedi Order fortunately escapes scrutiny is their African war lord-like child abduction. Throughout the tens of thousands of years, the Jedi have no problem exclusively recruiting child warriors with or without the consent of the parents. The children are taken at such a young age, they cannot remember their family lest they grow attachment to them which is against the Jedi Code. Yoda seems to attribute Anakin's falling away to his relationship with his mother. Remember, the Jedi are the good guys. Whether or not the child agrees to be brain washed and mercilessly trained and molded into the perfect Jedi warrior, they are expected to learn the ways of the Force day in and day out. All for the sake of peace and justice in the Galaxy, these child warriors may die for their moral cause. An army Koni must have idolized this use of child warriors if he has seen it.

Luke Skywalker is a huge agent for the Jedi cause, but the same train of thought should be focused on his actions in respects to the Force as a whole. Remember, both the Jedi and Sith had to be purged and in the time of Luke, there were only two Jedi masters left: Obi Wan Kenobi and Yoda both of whom Luke seemed to constantly butt heads with. Usually attributed to the master-apprentice relationship, the frustration grows. In the book, Luke completes a very difficult day-long task while Yoda narrates and criticizes. Finally, Luke, filled with joy, completed the task but is soon let down to hear from Yoda that yes, he completed the task, but he used his frustration to complete it. A back handed remark that reminds us the out dated Jedi mind set is still with the remaining Jedi.

The Empire Strikes Back is usually proclaimed as the best film. For Luke, it is the most important as he begins his more serious Jedi training but also begins the path away from the Jedi ways. First, when worried for his friends and in a storm of loyalty, passion, and urgency tells Yoda and Kenobi he has to pause his training save his friends. The old masters, worried for his safety and the future of their ways, strongly advised against it. Not only are they opposed to Luke's sense of loyalty and compassion, are also spiteful towards his free spirited individualism. These are of the dark side! We may quickly be reminded that the dark side is the human side and respects loyalty and compassion. But Yoda and Kenobi abandon this moral attribute for the sake of their philosophy (which, it has to be said, the only ones who truly want the Jedi order to return are the two surviving Jedi. If their plan to train Luke and pitch him against the Sith Lords fails, no one would know or care). The final objection to Luke's journey is from Obi Wan who threatens to not assist Luke if Luke gets into trouble. A life threatening claim is fulfilled when, faced with death, had to be saved in return by his friends. Kenobi would rather let Luke die than to put aside his Jedi code. Seems like even the Jedi trophy boy cannot trust in the Jedi assistance. This is seen in comparison where the Sith are seen to stop at nothing to step in to help friends and loved ones. Who would have thought the dark side has such a soft side. Please remember that Anakin's flight to the dark side was to save his wife and Reven's excommunication from the Jedi order was so that he could get married.

Luke stays vigilant to his own sense of morality by allowing marriage, free access to library archives, and a choice to join the order or not. It is out of the very idea of liberty and free thought that Luke integrated the best aspects of love, loyalty, and knowledge into his new Jedi order. Knowledge, being the biggest ideal in their code having been listed second, was ignored before Luke. The vast library the Jedi possessed was not available to everyone – and more seriously – not available to the lesser Jedi members. The oligarchy of the high Jedi masters reserved the right to restrict certain books and monitor the user's browsing. This is obviously another hypocritical condition of the Jedi and provides little room for any moral argument.

The Jedi, then, finishes the stripping of any individuality but outlawing emotions. How totalitarian can one get and still be the protagonists in a series? It would seem Mussolini and Franco have some work to do to catch up to the Jedi in that respect. The only thing the Order is missing is thought crime – but ha! Mind control. Who else but the Jedi would be able to read and control minds? Maybe the definition of knowledge isn't the spread of knowledge but the control of it. Rightly parallel to the Sith, who have no mention of knowledge in their code, strive for knowledge. It is widely known that the Sith Lords, in an attempt to escape death, create hollocrons which are used to store all that they have learned. The quest is dangerous and is always shared with their apprentice, and in the case of the early Sith, shared with the students of the Jedi order.

In respects to liberty, love, emotions altogether, loyalty, censorship, and knowledge the Jedi stand with those such as Kim Jun-il, Joseph Stalin, and Adolf Hitler (especially in regards to genocide). Some readers maybe reduced to the last argument to be made of the Jedi: that the Sith are obviously bad, why not just side with the Jedi? The last speck of the irrational mind pulls the viewer to think "at least they are trying to do what's best". Maybe one can see where I'm headed. The noble actions of many who appear or proclaim to be just have always doomed human history. Can we be reminded of the Nazi SS in this case? If I could dissect what little emotion the SS barbarians have, then we could begin seeing the foundation of the Jedi. Holy missions, such as the crusades and the Spanish Inquisition, have also used these arguments to justify their backward thinking. I beg you to always be vigilant when you meet a faction who claims to have all the answers, because the Jedi looms behind this fantastic idea of a utopia. At least the Sith actually follow up with their promises.

It is absolutely silly to use this much effort and apply this much time to analyzing a fictional order like the Jedi, but I strongly believe that, out of human nature, we assume too much in people's' characteristics. We jump to conclusions and assume the Jedi are ideal. This cannot be further from the case! It is of a health mind to question these things, for fun or for the protection of the truth. I challenge the reader the exercise and appeal to this natural contrarian thought process.

December 7, 2016

The Good and The Bad: Donald Trump so Far

At least half of the country would feel a small twitch of frustration when they see "good" and "Trump" in the same sentence. Donald Trump has defiantly ruffed some feathers and caused some stress in our country lately – even in me! I did not vote for the man, but I am please (so far) with what I have seen. Remember: Trump isn't even president yet and he is doing far more than any other president-elect, creating a hopeful future for his administration. Whether you like him or not, credit should be recognized where it is due, and for someone I previously described as a "complete buffoon", Trump has impressed me. I hope two things: Americans keep an open mind to his work and that Trump stays this busy to avoid any foot-in-mouth situations.

The biggest surprise to me is the eye-opening Carrier deal. When I saw the news that Donald Trump made a deal with the air conditioning country, I had to verify it and found it was true! Of course, some may say "he did not save all jobs at Carrier" – but those same people refuse to acknowledge that Trump is not president. He has no commitment to get to work already. Note that it is President Obama's job to try and save these jobs. Trump's loud speeches about negotiation trade deals seems to have some substance – but something else begs attention about this accomplishment: Trump isn't the brainless, flamboyant, tough-guy we thought he was. Trump is honestly taking this job seriously.

The next impressive move from Donald Trump is the active communication with foreign leaders. Obama did extend a hand (or, at times, bowed) to foreign leaders when he entered office – but again: that is when he was already on the payroll. The first, and probably most well thought out protest to this action is that Trump has not been briefed by the State Department yet. This protocol is followed so that the President knows the world affairs more thoroughly that the average citizen. Although it is hard to tell what they are discussing, we can assume that is has to do with negotiations and relations. So far, Donald Trump has called, visited, or spoke with:

Egyptian President Abdel Fattah el-Sisi, Australian PM Malcolm Turnbull, Irish PM Enda Kenny, Japanese PM Shinzo Abe, Israeli PM Benjamin Netanyahu, Canadian PM Justin Trudeau, Mexican President Enrique Pena Nieto, Saudi Arabian King Salman bin Abdulaziz Al-Saud, and Turkish President Recep Tayyip Erdogan (on the first day as President Elect)

Since day one, Trump has also come in contact with:

German Chancellor Angela Merkel, Italian PM Matteo Renzi, British PM Theresa May, S. Korean President Park Geun-hye, French President Francois Hollande, Chinese President Xi Jinping, Argintinan Presdient Mauricio Macri, Russian President Vladimir Putin (first time meeting him), Ukraine President Petro Poroshenko, and Dannish PM Lars Lokke Rasmussen to name a few. The meetings have not stopped except to save jobs, but that factor has been overlooked. It is important for anti-Trumpers to realize: yes, call him out on his deplorable comments, but use some critical thinking – Trump is in fact doing good and this communication is a unique Trump characteristic that hints at a very productive administration.

This communication has already seen some benefits. Japanese business man Masayoshi Son has met with Donald Trump and negotiated a deal in which Son and his company SoftBank will invest $50 billion in the United Sates with the objective to create 50,000 new jobs. The details are few but so is anxiety that Trump will some how make himself a debtor to foreign countries. Mana Nakazora, the chief credit analyst echos other's concerns, "I think Son must have thought how to use Trump and this opportunity". Yes, it is fair to wonder what this deal entails, but it is also reasonable to think that Trump is not afraid to dump anyone who think thy can get a favor from Trump. Election year 2016 – need I say more? The deal does speak volumes toward Trumps supposed negotiation skills, "Masa said he would never do this had we (Trump) not won the election!"

Finally, there is the stock market: the lifeline of the economy. The more poetic business writers describe the bulls and bears of Wall Street as the heartbeat of the country. Following that relationship, the shock of election day reflects the people's shell shock response to Trump. Note that stock market shocks on election day are common and Trump's was not as bad as his predecessors. MSNBC and CNN Money have both echoed other declarations that a Trump win would devastate the economy. The warmest predictions have shown at least, " an 8% fall in the U.S. A new paper out Friday from the Brookings Institute projects a 10% to 15% nosedive" These predictions and many others, though semi-rational due to Trump's air of uncertainty, are probably the most laughable of all. In fact, the DOW Jones Average broke all-time records by breaking the 19000 mark and even close to 20,000. This reaction is not directly Trump, but is the confidence of Trump perceived by the public. If that is the case, we have little to fear.

There are more dissenter than fans of Trump in the media, and they have so far ignored the accomplishments while working overtime to try and find some negatives about Trump. Those negatives have not changed since election day. In The Slates "230 Things Donald Trump Has Said and Done That Make Him Unfit to Be President", one can see that there is little substance in the case against Donald Trump other than his rhetoric – which is a definite issue. But the feelings of Hillary supporter's should not have any bearing on Trump's actions. When someone barks, "that's offensive!" the rational minded replies, "I am still waiting to hear your point" Actions speak louder than words, and although it is hard to imagine anything being louder than Trump's words, his actions provide solid evidence for a much better president than I or most American's could have expected. Yes, he seems to have stirred the already tense racial and socioeconomic conditions. But, when one studies the recent #notmypresident protests, the real cause for tensions become apparent.

My advice: take a breath, have a drink, and do some research – the future is no as bleak as we are lead to believe.

December 10, 2016

The Little Skeptic: My Favorite Skeptic Children's Books

Among the millennials, there seems to be a trend towards a child-free life. The baffling part about this, they seem to be proud of it! I know, they are free to do, think, say anything they want, but it is important to be mindful about the skeptical movement as a whole. If one wanted to make a difference – raising one of your own is the best way. And while I respect a child-free life style because it is a lot of responsibility and take a lot of resources away from you (See *The Selfish Gene* by Richard Dawkins) – but I beg my comrades to consider the incredible work secular couples are ding for the future. Plus, the world seems far too full of credulous parents anyways.

I recently had my first child – a happy baby girl. It is true what Christopher Hitchens said about his, "…three delightful children who are everything to me and who are my only chance of even a glimpse of a second life, let alone an immortal one…" This little girl is more important to me than anything I could ever imagine. I still get that cold shiver when I hold back tears imaging the infinite amounts of opportunists that are available for my little girl. The rest of Hitchen's quote begs to be said, "…and I'll tell you something: if I was told to sacrifice them to prove my devotion to God, if I was told to do what all monotheists are told to do and admire the man who said, 'Yes, I'll gut my kid to show my love of God,' I'd say, 'No. Fuck you.'" Needless to say, no rational parent would admit to be like Abraham, but alas, there are an abundance of irrational parents. We are surrounded by them – and surrounded by propaganda aimed toward children. Realizing this, I wanted to select my own propaganda that aims my baby towards open mindedness, skepticism, and happiness. In the Secular social network site, the secularnest.com, I have seen people trying to find acceptable baby books. Here is a list of my favorite baby so far!

1. *What do you do with an Idea?* by Kobi Yamada

Like all children's books, What do you do with an Idea include incredibly beautiful pieces of art to accompany the protagonist's journey about dealing with an idea. At first, our hero finds a little egg with small feet and a golden crown. The hero wonders about the idea and decides to ignore it – but the idea persists and he finally accepts the idea. he decides to hid the idea

> *"I worried what others would think. What would people say about my idea?"*

Our young hero grew closer to his idea and began playing with it. The idea is seen growing larger and larger. The heart breaking moment of the book is when the reader sees the child standing in front of a large group of adults. The reader is probably reminded of moments where they are scolded by parents or teachers. Like a child waiting at a bus stop on the first day of school, our hero presents his idea

> *"I showed it to other people even though I was afraid of what they would say. I was afraid they would laugh at it. I was afraid they would think it was silly. And many of them did. They said it was no good. They said it was too weird. They said it was a waste of time and that it would never become anything."*

The solemn depiction of the child walking away from his now large idea is shown. Any parent will feel daggers in their hearts when the hero says

"And, at first, I believed them. I actually thought about giving up on my idea. I almost listened to them"

The child realizes that the adults really don't know what they are talking about and tends to his idea. The Idea teaches him to dream, to think bigger, and how to see things differently. The book comes to a close as the idea becomes so big it bursts and fills the page with warm colors. And the book ends in the most beautiful way possible: the boy learns that

"[The Idea] wasn't just a part of me anymore. It was now a part of everything. And then I realized what you do with an idea: You change the world"

See the book here

2. *I Wonder* by Annaka Harris

Yes, that is Harris as in neuroscience, skeptic, and secular extraordinaire: Sam Harris. And just like Sam Harris, *I Wonder* is filled with beautiful lessons about admitting sometimes you don't know the answer, but that allows you to wonder about it and grow – not knowing even provides the rich opportunity in the background of all human advancements: the opportunity to wonder together with each other.

In the book, the little girl – whose name is coincidentally close to my own daughter's name – walks with her mother at night and questions many amazing questions: life cycles, gravity, and the vastness of the cosmos to name a few. But the daughter learns to most important lesson of all: sometimes you (or adults for that matter) knows the answer to something. And that is a great thing

"The moon looks so beautiful in the sky. How do you think it follows us, Eva?

Eva thinks about it, but she just can't figure it out. "It's okay to say, I don't know," says her mother. When we don't know something, we get to wonder about it!"

Though the story is beautiful and the illustrations illuminating, the real meat of the purpose is found in the author's note where the reader can see some of her husband in her:

"We live in a society where people are uncomfortable with not knowing. Children aren't taught to say 'I don't know' and honesty in this form is rarely modeled for them, They too often see adults avoiding the questions and fabricating the answers, out of either embarrassment or rear, and this comes at a price."

3. *Star Stuff: Carl Sagan and the Mysteries of the Cosmos* by Stephanie Roth Sisson

This book is actually about the late scientist Carl Sagan and follows his own eyeopening adventure to wonder. Star Stuff starts with a young Carl Sagan watching the stars from his bedroom window and wondering one of the oldest questions in human history: What are they? The lesson and the hopes of this book is to encourage your child to never stop questioning.

The book opens to a beautiful Milky Way and begins to put the cosmos into prospective. This is just one way the book forces the parent and child to begin discussing the vast cosmos. The possibilities are endless for a young mind. In fact, I still remember reading a book about space with my father. We sat down and read Exploring the Night Sky: The Equinox Astronomy Guide for Beginners by Terence Dickinson – It lead me to question what we were reading and interact with my dad. A more sweet moment from the book is when I did not believe light was the fastest in the Universe (I was pretty young). To prove it, my dad stood at one end of our apartment and flicked the lights on and I was to try and"beat" the light to the other end of the hallway. Although I tried several times, I couldn't beat it. Star Stuff is aimed towards younger children than Exploring the Night Sky, but it begs the same interaction between the parent and child. I can't wait to re-read this to my little girl and have those same mind-expanding moments with her.

Just as wondrous as staring at the stars, the reader is left to wonder: what if everyone wondered without ceasing? How many problems would be solved? How much more happiness could we obtain be grasping at real answers rather than settling with credulous beliefs? And then one remembers that your child is growing and wondering. It makes my mission so much more profound. Never stop wondering.

4. *The Giving Tree* by Shel Silverstein

The very first comedy I read was Shel Silverstein books such as A light in the Attic and Where the Sidewalk Ends. But I have neglected his most famous book of all – the 1964 classic The Giving Tree. I finally read it and was moved by the story but could not really place my finger on what was so touching.

For those who haven't read it, the story is there is "the Boy" and "the Tree" who, in the Boy's youth, were best friends. The boy played on the Tree and ate her apples and enjoyed himself. Soon, the Boy begins to grow and becomes interest in girls and money. The Boy starts to go to the Tree and asks for material things. First, The Boy asks for money, and the Tree offers all her apples so he can sell them. He does so, does not thank the tree, and after each deed, the Tree is happy. Next, The Boy needs a house for his wife and child, so the Tree gives him her branches to build the house. Then, the boy is much older and seemingly retired – desires to get away. The Tree gives him her entire trunk to make a canoe to sail around the world in. One cannot soon forget the sight of that page where the tree is now bear down to the stump leaving only the "Boy + T" heart carved into the tree. Finally, the Boy, now a hobbling old man, comes back and the Tree proudly offers the stump as a place to sit.

What could all of this mean? Being such an old book, there are vast amounts of theories online. The most apparent one that comes to me is Man's relationship with Nature. In our infancy, we have a mutual relationship – but quickly drift away to more material things while taking from Nature. This seems a bit obvious to me – but then again, the book was written in the 60's. A popular alternative is that The Giving Tree is about the beauty of generosity with a twist of dark ungratefulness. It is often thought that children get there morals from their parents, teachers, religion, or friends. Luckily, this is not the case. Like survival, social and mathematics skills, children are shown to be born with an innaite sense of morality and this book provides a story of giving and loss to expose children to this evolutionary trait. Elissa Straus of The Week explains this perfectly:

> *"It's the misguided belief that children can't recognize the sadness or the darkness behind the caregiver relationship that pushes many to misread this story as a happy one. But children can."*

That is all I have for now. Keep in mind, my daughter is a newborn and cannot really absorb the invaluable lessons in these books, but I read anyway to bond with her and for her to hear my voice. Because hearing parent's voices is so valuable to newborns, I suggest reading as soon as possible. It can even be adult books! If I find anymore astounding children's books and if this post does well, I may post more books. Until then, feel free to leave a comment recommending any other like-minded books for me.

December 13, 2016

Fact Checking – The Newest Trend

Keeping in mind that the internet is a relatively new invention for us. People are constantly becoming more and more connected and sharing information at a pace never before seen on Earth. But in a billboard-like way, news articles are trying to get attention anyway possible. Social Networking sites like Facebook do not help by condensing facts and stories down to a few sentences. The connectivity of the world and the need for quick and easy information has finally accumulated to a new type of propaganda - and we are finally fighting back.

It seems most have heard about fact checking articles and people in the 2016 presidential debate when Hillary Clinton imitated a crow and barking, "fact checkers!" every 5 minutes. And although we need to fact check everything, many use "fact check" as an argument - because no one will fact check it. It is far too hard to continuously fact check and research statements and studies. How would one know if they can even trust a new article anymore? There was a journalist who, when asked why he became a journalist, responded, "So I don't have to rely on others for news". A good response - but the average person does not have time to fact check, research, interpenetrate, and respond - until now!

There are plenty of fact checking sites that have always been around, but with the recent fake news, has been becoming more and more popular. because fake news articles have a propaganda-esc feel to them, the respond to clicks and clicks are because of fear and anger. Such has happened last week when Edgar Maddison opened gun fire at a Comet Ping Pong pizzaaria because of a fake news article. (1) Yes, people actually died! What was the fake article? It's called Pizzagate (2).Pizzagate alledges that there are a number of pizzarias in Washington D.C. that are secretly a part of a child sex ring. The sex ring is used by big-wig Democrats and apparently set up by Hillary Clinton herself. The fake news has already been debunked by multiple organizations - but if one simple used a second of critical thinking, you too could debunk it.

I appeal to the fair mindedness of my readers and assume little credulity. But, with social networking, one comes across plenty of brain-rotting articles that you know are false but need some links to prove it. Here are my favorite fact-checking sites. A fact is the strongest weapon against our gullible comrades.

Snopes

Founded in 1995, snopes.com handles the most common myths as well as social media myths. The way it works is that people send in rumors or myths and the team there researches it. The result is a concise and fact-heavy article with a clear True/ False/ or Nor Verifiable

FactCheck

Factcheck.org is a project created by the Annenberg Public Policy Center at the University of Pennsylvania. This site focuses around claims made by politicians, their speeches, and even TV ads. Their goal is to "apply the best practices of both journalism and scholarship, and to increase public knowledge and understanding"

Politifact

Politifact is an older but an increasingly popular site which won the Pulitzer Prize for researching 750 claims during the 2008 election. This site fact checks almost any political claims from politicians to advocacy groups. The results of their research results in a Truth-O-Meter rating that reads Truth, Mostly true, half True, False, and Pants on Fire.

But the best source is your own brain! Of course, these fake articles and myths appeal to our human flaws, but there is a tool you can use to investigate any claim and get a feel for its accuracy. It is called the Baloney Detection Kit: A 10-point checklist used by truth seeking organizations such as the Richard Dawkins Foundation for Reason and Science, Skeptic Magazine, and even the Daily Skeptic Blog! The check list, as shared by Skeptic Society found, Michael Shermer, is as follows:

Baloney Detection Kit

1. How reliable is the source of the claim?
2. Does the source make similar claims?
3. Have the claims been verified by someone else?
4. Does this fit with the way the world works?
5. Has anyone tried to disprove the claim?
6. Where does the preponderance of evidence point?
7. Is the claimant playing by the rules of science?
8. Is the claimant providing positive evidence?
9. Does the new theory account for as many phenomena as the old theory?
10. Are personal beliefs driving the claim?

The sharper minds already have examples in mind that could be debunked by this checklist - maybe Scientology, near-death experiences, luck, pseudoscience, or anything on Facebook to name a few. The point is, humans always have had to hear stories or myths and determine True or False on their own. The only difference now is that we hear and read stories on such a massive scale, it is hard to sift through it all. Most probably don't want to investigate every claim they hear anyways -- and with these new tools, they don't have to.

December 14, 2016

The Republic [Abridged Book Review]

[NOTE: Originally written in college, this paper weighed in at 10 pages long. I decided to post it, but post an abridged version to spare the reader. The original date is July 14, 2012]

Throughout history, art of all forms have shaped every society in our world. Art has a major influence on people - especially the youth. In order to ensure a better future the youth of a civilization must be raised correctly by their society with good influences. Plato's book *The Republic*, in a line of dialogue between Socrates and other men depicts the best ideals that would make the perfect society. In these discussions, Socrates addresses quickly what is wrong with education and what should be acceptable considered acceptable education standards to prepare societies youth to live in his Republic - but he also speaks on a more sensitive issue. Socrates addresses the control of art in this Republic to better the citizens within it. It maybe because Socrates has not lived through communism or nationalism, but one must admit: he is far ahead of his time. Although Socrates proves successful in pointing out flaws in poetry, drama, and all art - he fails to provide a realistic solution to the problems. He foretells and answers artistic flaws within the dialogue, but gives possible solutions as opposed to a plausible solutions.

Beginning in "Book II" of The Republic, Plato begins to write the discussion explaining how important it is to raise children correctly because they are so very impressionable. Socrates begins this discussion asking, "Shall we begin the education with music, and go to gymnastics afterwards?" - showing that the education he is referring to is younger education at an elementary base. He describes these children as young and tender things impressionable to the world in danger of misinterpretation to the stories that are told to them. One immediately begin to think about the crazy things children are exposed to - any reader can agree that the youth are impressionable and need some kind of direction in their education to insure they are raised to be their best. Imagine, for example, that every child is raised in something crazy such as Scientology. Socrates deserves credit for bringing this to the discussion because this will be a problem debated for thousands of years to come.

Even today, parents, scholars, and politicians fight over what children of today can see, hear, and do. Socrates makes the point that society cannot, "just carelessly allow children to hear any casual tales which may be devised by casual persons and to receive into their minds ideas for the most part the very opposite of those which we should wish them to have when they grow up". Religion comes to mind. Every parent, religious or not, wants their child exposed to the 'right' religion and protected from the wrong one. Keep in mind that Socrates was eventually put to death for corrupting the youth and questioning the gods. This could be where that claim against Socrates starts.

The fear is a primal one: that someone or something my corrupt one's child and ruin them for life. The 20th century children comes to mind as the struggle for artistic freedom in the 1960's and 1970's anti-war movement. The sort of art brought rebellion against the state and its efforts ultimately leading to the failure of the Vietnam war. But this cultural revolution not only brought about a split in loyalty in the State but also brought changes that shocked parents with drug use, violence, and a chaotic society.

This sort of change is exactly what Socrates is warning against. The dangers of the arts and allowing art to run free is considered anarchy for the State and its children. Now, our idea of the individual didn't really come around until the 1700's with Hobbes, Locke, and the American and French Revolution - so what Socrates is explaining was not so crazy - for the time. But these relatively recent individual liberty liberties is what Socrates would call a big lie, "A fault which is most serious, I said: the fault of telling a lie, and, what is more, a bad lie". All things considered, Socrates is correct for his concern for youth's influences within a society when one thinks about the vast amounts of misinformation and propaganda within our society today. Socrates provides the reader a legitimate problem that will reoccur for thousands of years. The solution for this problem is simply censorship. Today, we understand man's ability for discretion, but Socrates' plan is centered toward iron fisted censorship, "the first things will be to establish a censorship of writers of fiction and let the censors receive any tale of fiction with is good and reject the bad". This solution is possible - but not plausible. Simply think of any number of authoritarian dictatorships throughout history. Even if the reader assumes that the censorship of writers is possible and can function flawlessly, the people of the State would never allow it. Think of the resistance in Nazi Germany to receive foreign radio, in the Soviet Union to receive books, in Communist China to write whatever you want, even North Korea where the largest illegal imports are films. Even though Socrates' goal is a good one and means well, it would be too hard on a nation and it's people to enforce it - and we are not even talking about the intellectual depression a nation will face with censorship.

In Book III and Book IV, Socrates begins to again attack art but this time at its core. Socrates is mostly concerned with productivity of the Republic as it is most important for the State and its people, "the arts of measuring and numbering and weighing come to the rescue of the human understanding - there is the beauty of them". This aspect of Socrates' discussion is very insightful and well thought. If there were a type of Utopia attainable, it would need constant intellectual support from its people mainly presiding in something more useful such as math, science, and other trades - not art. Plus if these trades are necessary for the growth of the state then the time and skill of the citizens cannot be wasted on such useless trades such as art, "one man can only do one thing well, and not many; and that if he attempt many, he will altogether fail of gaining much reputation in any." Socrates would have loved - or be completely horrified by our Utopian books such as George Orwell's 1984 or Ayn Rand's Anthem. Perhaps he would have changed his mind about the individual's place within the State. He does, however grim, provides an explanation of human nature and if a perfect society needed trades from its people, they would need to be as productive as possible.

After the production of society is handled, Socrates then moves onto the influences of art and recognizes that art influences every single person in society indiscriminately. Whether is from television, music, theater or painting, there is no avoiding some form of art. And if that was true in Classical Greece, imagine Socrates if he saw how much we are exposed to! Socrates points out that it is not stories citizen's should be concerned with, but rather good people with a good character, "if they imitate at all, they should imitate from youth upward only those characters which are suitable to their professions- the courageous, temperate, holy, free, and the like; but they should not depict or be skillful at imitation of any kind of illiberality or baseness". Not only does Socrates suggest censoring people's work, but the State should also provide examples for it's people -

propaganda. Yes, there is such a thing as unhealthy exposures to our children, but it is not up to the State to decide the ideal citizen.

As a mindful reader, one should realize that Socrates has not experienced the libertarian movements we take for granted nor has he seen the horrors of fascist and communist dictatorships. With that being said, The Republic is still a classic thought provoking book that forces to reader to think about how society should run. The fight for liberty is unfortunately one that has to be fought in every generation. Though this book describes a authoritarian utopia - it is still a necessary book for us to read, wonder, and debate about.

December 15, 2016

Trump and Populism

Populism. It is everywhere in the news right now and it is one of those words that have so many vague meanings and yet describes itself so well. Populism is simply the revolt of the people against the political machine. With that said, the word perfectly matches what Trump supporters and haters think of Trump's new Republican Party. He won with the party and with the nation despite being resented by the Republican leaders and Washington elite. But where did the name Populist come from?

In the late 1800's, the southern and western farmers were struggling due to the industrialization and reconstruction after the Civil War. (1) The changing international markets, national banks, railroad companies made agricultural commerce difficult even though the farms still worked and produced goods. Those complications combined with the southern dissent from the Civil War accumulated to the Populist movement. The movement was slow-moving but started with the Patrons of Husbandry or the "Grange". This group was more of a union of farmers that pooled money together to buy equipment and sway political power. There was even a Colored Farmers Alliance organization that branched off of the Grange. The organization brought poor farmers together: they did not represent the Democrats or the Republicans, they represented the marginalized farmers. Thus, the Populist movement was born. (2)

The Populist Party tried to gather some sort of political power in 1896 - but since they were outnumbered and out financed, they decided to join forces with the Democratic nominee William Jennings Bryan. This gave the Democrats a chance to finally win back the White House from the North and for the common man. Bryan seemed almost like Bernie Sanders when he speaks about the oppression of the rich, "You shall not press down upon the brow of labor this crown of thorns; you shall not crucify mankind upon a cross of gold!" Of course, Bryan did lose to McKinley, but the idea of the Populist movement was alive and well throughout the 1920's - as well as, some would argue - today with Donald Trump's Republican Party.

At the North American leader's summit, President Obama did not seem to approve of people calling Trump a Populist, "That's nativism. Or Xenophobia, or worse. Or it's just cynicism". (3) Yes, there are some Trump supporters who would subscribe to the nativism and xenophobia - but not most. I say also say the say about Populism. Michael Kazin describes Populism in his book "The Populist Persuasion" as, "a language whose speakers conceive of ordinary people as a noble assemblage not bounded narrowly by class, view their elite opponents as self-serving and undemocratic, and seek to mobilize the former against the latter".

So on its face; yes Trump does aim to be a Populist. But is this a good thing? Populists are sometimes known as being anti- science and anti-progressive. Although they seem to be very opposed to change, Populists do represent a class that is usually overlooked. In the end, words are just words - let's wait until Trump gets into office before we really start labeling the President Elect.

December 16, 2016

What Caused World War Two?

The cause of the Second World War is something that is hard to talk about. It is something that, if one thinks they know the answer, they will not listen to any new evidence. As you read this, you no doubt have already thought of how World War II started: German aggression, Hitler, Pearl Harbor, Japanese aggression, the Tripartite Pact. While they are all true, some more than others, one must first start a little further back in history. Before the Third Reich, before the Japanese Empire began its war march, before Hitler. Let's begin with the accumulation of industrial colonial powers that led to the First World War.

The beginning of World War One is attributed to the web of alliances and influences across Europe set afire with one assassination. First, Arch Duke Ferdinand was assassinated by a disgruntled Serbian in 1914. In a flash of rage, the Austro-Hungarian Empire declared war against the tiny Serbian nation. The Russian Empire, looking for influence in the region had promised to protect Serbia and declared war against the Austro-Hungarian Empire. Austro-Hungarian Germanic brothers, the newly formed German Empire, took up arms against the Russians. The French were allies with the Russian Empire and declared war against the Germans. The Germans declared was against Belgium to go around France and attack at a better point. Belgium fell quickly but pulled Great Britain into the fray. Later, the Americans were provoked when they intercepted a German sub trying to bring Mexico into a war to retake their lost land from the United States. Yes, it is a bit confusing and I admit I simplified it tremendously. It helps of you drew a map of the conflict but keep in mind there are many other players in the war (The Ottomans, Italians, Japan, and others).

After years of fighting, the First World War came to a bloody and depressing stalemate - the very first large scale trench war. The European fighters were relieved when the United States came into the war forcing the Germans into an unconditional surrender. Peace treaties now a days are relatively forgiving compared to the peace treaty for World War I. Every nation on every side was mad, weary, and bitter. There were one million British dead, one million seven hundred thousand Frenchmen gone, four hundred sixty thousand Italians gone, and over one million seven hundred thousand Russians and Turks dead - making it far too easy for revenge to seep its way into the peace treaty - the dreaded Treaty of Versailles.

Although the Treaty of Versailles ended the First World War, it brought an unsettled fire to Germany - one that will be stoked and used by Adolf Hitler to come to power. It was not the aggression by Hitler or the authoritarian dictators across the world that started the war - it was the brutal Treaty of Versailles. And many historians are slowly coming to the same conclusion. A.J.P. Taylor claimed that, "If this [German problem] were settled, everything would be settled; if it remained unsolved, Europe would not know peace" The only thing the treaty accomplished was a short-term relief to the Allies, and a podium for Hitler and Nazi Germany to rise to power.

The Treaty reduced the German army to no larger than one hundred thousand men, eliminated their air force, submarines, and most heavy surface vehicles, stripped Germany of Alsace-Lorraine, Danzig, and other territorial land - but even with this castration of the once proud German people - the most outrageous and suppressing part of the treaty was Article 231, also known as the war guilt clause which stated

"The Allied and Associated Governments affirm and Germany accepts the responsibility of Germany and her allies for causing all the loss and damage to which that Allies and Associated Governments and their nationals have been subjected as a consequence of the war imposed upon them by the aggression of Germany and her allies"

It held Germany completely responsible for the war, the war damages, and deaths from the first catastrophic war - but because the Germans suffered over two million deaths and were completely stretched thin - the German leaders bit their lip and signed the Treaty. Signing the treaty then was completely pointless because the Allies already negotiated the Treaty on the eleventh hour of the eleventh day of the eleventh month - and signed it without any German representative. In the aftermath of the war, Former Chancellor of Germany, Franz von Papen, captured the feelings of all Germans saying, "The grave errors and injustices contained in the Versailles treaty can only be explained by the state of hysteria engendered in the Allied Powers by years of hate-filled and untrue propaganda." There were a good amount of Allies who thought the same thing. Winston Churchill remarked, "All sorts of races who counted for nothing, or stood aside from, or were protected in the dire struggle of the world, hurried up with their pretensions while the great combatants la gasping. Then came the period which was easy to predict, when the victors forgot and the vanquished remembered"

So, the Germans lay in defeat and stripped of any real power. The reparations they owed to the Allies kept them suppressed and unable to gain any sort of power. The decades of poverty only resulted in Hitler's claim to power - which he got legally. He was voted into power because the German people were looking for any hope - hope that they would not find abroad. Prime Minister of the United Kingdom, Lloyd George, expressed the attitude of the victors by suggesting they, "Squeeze Germany until the pips squeak". And the Allies meant it - Germany didn't pay off their massive debt until October of 2010. The fuel for the fire - the Rage of the Reich - is used by Adolf Hitler over and over to rally the German people who, desperate for relief, carried Hitler's banner. Hitler denounced all debt from the Treaty of Versailles in 1933 declaring this ghastly statement

"It is not wise to deprive a people of the economic resources necessary for its existence without taking into consideration the fact that the population dependent on them are bound to the soil and will have to be fed. The idea that the economic extermination of a nation of sixty-five millions would be of service to other nations is absurd. Any people inclined to follow such a line of thought would, under the law of cause and effect, soon experience that the doom which they were preparing for another nation would swiftly overtake them. The very idea of reparations and the way in which they were enforced will become a classic example in the history of the nations of how seriously international welfare can be damaged by hasty and unconsidered action...

December 17, 2016

Russian Hack Investigation

Former Presidential Candidate Hillary Clinton seems to want to end her biggest run of her life with the biggest lie of her life. Mrs. Clinton started with an attack towards rival Donald Trump alleging that he is spreading conspiracy theories and smearing our election process (which is true) – but now she is claiming that her shady emails where leaked by Russia. She came up with this theory quickly after the emails were leaked – making the election all the more juicy. The biggest let down from this whole conspiracy is that we, the voter, have never heard any proof. Even the electoral college members wanted a briefing before they voted, and received none. So is there any truth behind the Russian Conspiracy?

Let's recap. Beginning in the Democratic Primaries, emails from the Democratic National Committee and Clinton were leaked to Wikileaks. The topics of the emails are dark and shady ranging from racist comments to actually conspiring against Bernie Sanders to ensure Clinton's victory. (1) Even though the emails were legit, Hillary and the DNC cried foul. So it seems that you can be corrupt and vindictive as long as it is in an email. (2)

Fast forward past Clinton's and Trump's victory and more emails are released revealing the sinister workings of the Democratic party. And just as Trump can do anything without blame, Clinton avoided any blame for her emails because she alleged that the Russians hacked her – no mention of her private email server where anyone could probably hacked and no mention of the possibility that a DNC staffer or a Bernie supporter might have leaked the emails (Imagine that person watching the news as everyone thinks Russia leaked the emails). No, Clinton went straight to a Cold War era conspiracy – and now everyone is buying into it without any sort of evidence. No one seemed to make much noise over the claim until Hillary actually lost – then half the country, including President Obama and government agencies started investigating.

Now, imagine for a moment: half the country, the White House, and the FBI and CIA are trying to find proof – and trying to bar Trump from the White House. If this sort of power found evidence of Russian hackers, wouldn't it benefit them and be a huge moral responsibility to notify us? What are they waiting for? Just recently, the CIA director John Brennan reported, "Earlier this week, I met separately with FBI [Director] James Comey and DNI Jim Clapper, and there is strong consensus among us on the scope, nature, and intent of Russian interference in our presidential election"(3) Both directors and agencies refused to comment on that report. But is there a better time to come our and stop Trump than today? Today is that last chance with the Electoral College voting.

Not only did the Electoral College voter beg for a briefing on the Russian investigation, but Trump, and Wikileaks, and Russia, and half of America is begging for some sort of evidence. (4) Wikileaks even offered to host the evidence, "Obama should submit any Putin documents to Wikileaks to be authenticated to our standards if he wants them to be seen as credible" (5) Russian Presidential Spokesman Dmitry Peskov said it was, "indecent of the United States to groundlessly accuse Russia of intervention in the US election campaign" Mr. Peskov continues, "They should either stop talking about that or produce some proof at last. Otherwise it all begins to look unseemly" (6)

Yes, there seems to be some friendship between Trump and Putin – but Trump has dozens of other foreign friendships just as capable to hack into emails. And yes, there is no doubt Putin would rather have Trump in the White House than Clinton. But that has no bearing on if the claim is true. I, and any reasonable reader want to know what really happened. Maybe someone needs to hack their emails to figure what is going on in our own country. Any claim asserted without evidence can be dismissed without evidence – and I hope we see some evidence soon.

Now, I am posting this as my last post of the year as I take an hiatus over the holidays. So if it comes out that Russia really did hack the DNC emails – I will be the first to admit that. But keep in mind, whoever hacked the emails, Clinton and the DNC still said all those things. They really conspired against members of their own party. They still betrayed and miss presented their own voters. And Clinton still challenged our election system without revealing her proof.

Be on the lookout for one of two possibilities: it is proven that Russia has hacked our election, or Clinton is a liar. If the trend proves consistent – it is far more likely to be the later of the two.

Statistics for the Daily Skeptic Blog by the end of the first year of writing are recorded below:

Total Number of blog posts:	<u>70</u>
Total Number of views:	<u>586</u>
Total Number of Readers:	<u>359</u>

Top 10 blogs:

1) *Dr. Phillip Stetz – A Review*   September 19

2) What Happened at Wells Fargo?   September 26

3) The Jefferson Series   November 15

4) NDPL Misinformation   September 14

5) Condom Ban Hoax   August 30

6) The 5 Threats of Islam   September 28

7) My 2016 Presidential Election Prediction   October 20

8) Rigged Election: Can it be True?   September 2

9) Mike Pence the Credulous   August 11

10) Epipen Epidemic   August 27

References

NOTE: Many sources and links referenced throughout the essays contain videos, debates, transcripts, pictures, maps, and news reports. Although I have tried to include all sources used in the original posts, some have become unattainable from the original site used and have been omitted from the references section below. For original sources, visit dailyskepticblog.wordpress.com

August

Mike Pence the Credulous

(1) Congressional Record. (2002, July 11). Theory of the Origin of Man. Retrieved December 14, 2016, from Congress.gov, https://www.congress.gov/congressional-record/2002/7/11/house-section/article/h4527-1?q=%7B%22search%22%3A%5B%22%5C%22mike+pence%5C%22%22%5D%7D&resultIndex=190

(2) Gilgamesh, H. (2016, August 5). "Evolution is just A theory" - Mike Pence argues to congress - able to choose. Retrieved December 14, 2016, from Patheos.com, http://www.patheos.com/blogs/abletochoose/2016/08/mike-pence-evolution/

(3) Allen, B. (2006). Moral minority: Our skeptical founding fathers. Chicago: Dee, Ivan R. Publisher.

Closet Sexists

RWW Blog (2016, August 12). Bryan Fischer says "I don't believe that women should be entrusted with high political office" Retrieved from https://youtu.be/idoJcUWMbYc

The 5000 Years Leap Backwards

(1) Skousen, C. W. (2007). The 5000 year leap (original authorized edition) [8 disk set]. Malta, ID: National Center for Constitutional Studies.

(2) Christopher Hitchens (2012, September 12). Grand Vallet State Univseristy, 2010 Retrieved from https://www.youtube.com/watch?v=-KJMNv-8sfw

Student Loan Forgiveness

Bass, K. (2016, June 28). Student Loan Fairness act. Retrieved December 14, 2016, from bass.house.gov, https://bass.house.gov/bill/student-loan-fairness-act

Nuclear Energy Misinformation

(1) Stein, Jill. https://twitter.com/drjillstein/status/715230945679380481. 10:35, March 30, 2016

(2) Rinkesh. (2015, April 28). 30 facts about nuclear energy - conserve energy future. Retrieved December 14, 2016, from Nuclear, http://www.conserve-energy-future.com/various-nuclear-energy-facts.php

(3) Finley, R. (2015, December 02). Bill Nye the Science Guy Social Primate and Nuclear Energy. Retrieved December 14, 2016, from http://www.energytrendsinsider.com/2015/12/02/bill-nye-the-science-guy-social-primate-and-nuclear-energy/http://www.nirs.org/factsheets/plutbomb.htm

US Science and Math Scores on the Rise

Brown, E. (2015, October 28). U.S. Student performance slips on national test. Washington Post. Retrieved from https://www.washingtonpost.com/local/education/us-student-performance-slips-on-national-test/2015/10/27/03c80170-7cb9-11e5-b575-d8dcfedb4ea1_story.html

The Power of Prayer

(1) Carey, B. (2015, February 17). Long-awaited medical study questions the power of prayer. Health. Retrieved from http://www.nytimes.com/2006/03/31/health/31pray.html?_r=0
(2) News, S. (2006, March 30). Power of prayer flunks an unusual test. Retrieved December 14, 2016, from Heart health, http://www.nbcnews.com/id/12082681/ns/health-heart_health/t/power-prayer-flunks-unusual-test/#.V79unZgrLtQ
(3) Patheos Blog, (2009, May 15). Study concludes Intercessory prayer Doesn't work; Christians twist the results. Retrieved December 14, 2016, from Friendly Atheist, http://www.patheos.com/blogs/friendlyatheist/2009/05/15/study-concludes-intercessory-prayer-doesnt-work-christians-twist-the-results/
(4) G., & Fung, C. (2009, May 15). What do prayer studies prove? Retrieved December 14, 2016, from http://www.christianitytoday.com/ct/2009/may/27.43.html

Five Threats of Islam

Yiannopoulos, M. (2016, September 27). FULL TEXT: 10 things Milo hates about Islam. Retrieved December 14, 2016, from Breitbart, http://www.breitbart.com/milo/2016/09/27/10-things-milo-hates-islam/

The Mind of the Market

Shermer, M., & Shermer, M. (2007). The mind of the market: Compassionate apes, competitive humans, and other tales from evolutionary economics. New York: St Martin's Press.

September

Price of Civilization

(1) Brown, M. (2014). Penal Power and Colonial Rule (1st ed., p. 68, 69). Routledge.
(2) Cole, G., Smith, C. & Dejong, C. (2016). Criminal Justice in America. (8th Ed.) Cengage Learning: Boston.
(3) Dhawan, H., & Thakur, P. (2015, July 21). Here's proof that poor get gallows, rich mostly escape. Retrieved November 24, 2015, from http://timesofindia.indiatimes.com/india/Heres-proof-that-poor-get-gallows-rich-mostly-escape/articleshow/48151696.cms
(4) Hall, C. (n.d.). Jennifer Ertman & Elizabeth Pena – murder victims. Retrieved November 25, 2015, from http://www.murdervictims.com/voices/jeneliz.html
(5) Innocenceproject.org. (n.d.). Retrieved November 25, 2015, from http://www.innocenceproject.org/cases-false-imprisonment/marvin-anderson
(6) Figure 1. Innocenceproject.org (2013). The Causes of Wrongful Conviction, Retrieved from Innocenceproject.org (http://www.innocenceproject.org/causes-wrongful-conviction)
(7) Long, J. (1869). Unpublished Records of Government for the Years 1748-1767 Inclusive Relating Mainly to the Social Condition of Bengal (p. 224). Harvard University.
(8) Pataki, G. (1997, March 1). Death Penalty is a Deterrent. USA Today. Retrieved November 24, 2015.
(9) Raghavan, V. (2005, August 30). Of Mangal Pandey and the Madras Army. Retrieved November 25, 2015, from http://www.thehindu.com/2005/08/30/stories/2005083006941100.htm
(10) Tolkien, J. (1965). The Lord of the Rings: The Two Towers (2d ed.,ch. 2, pg. 85). Boston: Houghton Mifflin.
(11) Figure 2. Tucker, William. (2001). More Executions, Fewer Murders, Retrieved from Bimmerfest.com (http://www.bimmerfest.com/forums/showthread.php

Trumps Tax Return

(1) Reuters. (2016). Trump advisors spin tax writeoff for $916 million loss as proof of his "genius" at business. Retrieved December 14, 2016, from http://www.rawstory.com/2016/10/trump-advisors-spin-tax-writeoff-for-916-million-loss-as-proof-of-his-genius-at-business/
(2) Publication 536. Retrieved December 14, 2016, from irs.gov, https://www.irs.gov/publications/p536/ar02.html

Did Glenn beck Endorse Hillary Clinton?

(1) Mansour, R. (2016, October 10). Glenn Beck: Electing Hillary Clinton "is a moral, ethical choice." Retrieved December 14, 2016, from 2016 Presidential Race, http://www.breitbart.com/2016-presidential-race/2016/10/10/glenn-beck-electing-hillary-clinton-moral-ethical-choice/?utm_source=facebook&utm_medium=social

(2) Staff, A. (2016, October 11). Glenn Beck, conservative pundit, endorses Hillary Clinton for president. Retrieved December 14, 2016, from http://www.aol.com/article/news/2016/10/11/glenn-beck-conservative-pundit-endorses-hillary-clinton-president/21578993/

(3) Beck, G. (2016, October 11). I am neither endorsing nor voting for Hillary Clinton. Retrieved December 14, 2016, from http://www.glennbeck.com/2016/10/11/i-am-neither-endorsing-nor-voting-for-hillary-clinton/

What happened at Wells Fargo? [Update]

(1) Turner, M., & Bryan, B. (2016, October 12). Wells Fargo CEO John Stumpf is out after a scandal over fake accounts. Retrieved December 14, 2016, from Business Insider, http://www.businessinsider.com/wells-fargo-ceo-john-stumpf-out-2016-10

(2) Koren, J. R. (2016, October 12). Wells Fargo CEO retires amid accounts scandal and is replaced by a longtime company insider. Retrieved December 14, 2016, from http://www.latimes.com/business/la-fi-wells-fargo-stumpf-resigns-20161012-snap-story.html

No One Left to Lie To

Times, T. W. (2016). Hillary Clinton's long list of lies. Retrieved December 14, 2016, from http://www.washingtontimes.com/news/2016/jun/19/hillary-clintons-long-list-of-lies/

Rusty. (2015, November 20). The 7 wildest lies from Hillary Clinton. Retrieved December 14, 2016, from Facebook Feature, http://www.thepoliticalinsider.com/t-day-evergreen-7-wildest-lies-hillary-clinton/

All false statements involving Hillary Clinton. (2016). Retrieved December 14, 2016, from http://www.politifact.com/personalities/hillary-clinton/statements/byruling/false/?page=2

Hitchens, C. (2008, January 14). The case against Hillary Clinton. Retrieved December 14, 2016, from http://www.slate.com/articles/news_and_politics/fighting_words/2008/01/the_case_against_hillary_clinton.html

Giuliani Lies about Clinton

(1) Mathis-Lilley, B. (2016, October 12). Rudy Giuliani says he didn't see Hillary at ground Zero (update: Giuliani Retracts accusation, apologizes). Retrieved December 14, 2016, from http://www.slate.com/blogs/the_slatest/2016/10/12/rudy_giuliani_hillary_clinton_toured_ground_zero_together_on_sept_12.html

(2) News, A. (2016). ABC news. Retrieved December 14, 2016, from http://abcnews.go.com/Politics/wireStory/giuliani-wrongly-accuses-clinton-lying-911-42763969

(3) Schwartzman, P., & Terris, B. (2016, October 16). What happened to "America's mayor"? How Rudy Giuliani became trump's attack dog. Washington Post. Retrieved from https://www.washingtonpost.com/lifestyle/style/what-happened-to-americas-mayor-how-rudy-giuliani-became-trumps-attack-dog/2016/10/13/c6fdebd4-8fc1-11e6-9c85-ac42097b8cc0_story.html

Predicting the Presidential Election

(1) Stevenson, P. W. (2016, September 23). Trump is headed for a win, says professor who has predicted 30 years of presidential outcomes correctly. Washington Post. Retrieved from https://www.washingtonpost.com/news/the-fix/wp/2016/09/23/trump-is-headed-for-a-win-says-professor-whos-predicted-30-years-of-presidential-outcomes-correctly/

(2) Wright, D. (2016, August 29). Brexit leader Nigel Farage calls trump "the new Ronald Reagan." CNN. Retrieved from http://www.cnn.com/2016/08/29/politics/nigel-farage-praises-trump-rally/

Do Vaccines Cause Amish Autism?

(1) Wenger, O. K., McManus, M. D., Bower, J. R., & Langkamp, D. L. (2011). Underimmunization in Ohio's Amish: Parental fears are a greater obstacle than access to care. Article. doi:10.1542/peds.2009-2599

(2) Robinson, J. L., & Institute, H. (2010, May 22). International meeting for autism research: Prevalence rates of autism spectrum disorders among the old order Amish. Retrieved December 14, 2016, from https://imfar.confex.com/imfar/2010/webprogram/Paper7336.html

(3) Kasprak, A., & Internet. (2016, October 28). The Amish don't get autism? Retrieved December 14, 2016, from http://www.snopes.com/the-amish-dont-get-autism/

(4) Arsenal, A.-V. S. S. (2015, April 29). Vaccines DO cause autism-undeniable scientific proof. Retrieved December 14, 2016, from https://avscientificsupportarsenal.wordpress.com/2015/04/29/vaccines-do-cause-autism-undeniable-scientific-proof/

(5) CDC. (2015, November 23). Vaccines do not cause autism. Retrieved December 14, 2016, from http://www.cdc.gov/vaccinesafety/concerns/autism.html

Gullible Predictions

(1) Bol-shevik, T. (2016, September 28). Town yanks cross from Christmas tree, all hell breaks loose. Retrieved December 14, 2016, from http://www.wnd.com/

(2) Does bible code predict president Romney? (2016, December 14). Retrieved December 14, 2016, from http://www.wnd.com/2012/10/does-bible-code-predict-president-romney/

November

Shameful Anti-Trump Protests

(1) Retrieved December 14, 2016, from https://www.washingtonpost.com/national/higher-education/the-latest-police-san-diego-student-assaulted-over-faith/2016/11/10/af344f80-a77b-11e6-ba46-53db57f0e351_story.html

(2) Evon, D. (2016, November 9). FALSE: "We hate Muslims, we hate blacks" chanted at trump rally. Retrieved December 14, 2016, from http://www.snopes.com/trump-rally-chant/

(3) Hauser, C. (2016, November 4). Killing of Saudi student shakes Wisconsin college town. U.S.Retrieved from http://www.nytimes.com/2016/11/04/us/killing-of-saudi-university-student-shakes-wisconsin-city.html?action=click&contentCollection=U.S.&module=RelatedCoverage&region=EndOfArticle&pgtype=article

Jeffersonian Hate

(1) FoxNews.com (2016, November 14). President of university founded by Jefferson asked to not quote Jefferson. Fox News. Retrieved from http://www.foxnews.com/us/2016/11/14/president-university-founded-by-jefferson-asked-to-not-quote-jefferson.html

(2) Hallock, G. (2015, February 2). Thomas Jefferson and slavery. Retrieved December 14, 2016, from https://www.monticello.org/site/plantation-and-slavery/thomas-jefferson-and-slavery

(3) Coates, T.-N., & O'Brien, C. C. (2014, November 18). Thomas Jefferson: Radical and racist. . Retrieved from http://www.theatlantic.com/magazine/archive/1996/10/thomas-jefferson-radical-and-racist/376685/

Thomas Jefferson on Slavery

(1) Donald Trump is selling make America Great again Christmas ornaments for $149. (2016, November 23). Retrieved December 14, 2016, from http://theweek.com/speedreads/663775/donald-trump-selling-make-america-great-again-christmas-ornaments-149

(2) Hallock, G. (2015, February 2). Thomas Jefferson and slavery. Retrieved December 14, 2016, from https://www.monticello.org/site/plantation-and-slavery/thomas-jefferson-and-slavery

(3) Retrieved December 14, 2016, from https://www.monticello.org/site/plantation-and-slavery/thomas-jefferson-and-slavery#footnote5_lo25tfr

(4) Lincoln on Thomas Jefferson. (1964). Retrieved December 14, 2016, from https://www.nps.gov/liho/learn/historyculture/jefferson.htm

(5) Jefferson's views on slavery. Retrieved December 14, 2016, from http://www.poplarforest.org/jefferson/plantation-life/jeffersons-views-on-slavery/#.WDXCpbIrKUk

Thomas Jefferson's Scandal
(1) Library, & Services, T. The Jefferson - Hemings controversy - about -. Retrieved December 14, 2016, from http://digital.lib.lehigh.edu/trial/jefferson/
(2) Chronology - Henry S. Randall's letter to James Parton (1868). Retrieved December 14, 2016, from http://www.pbs.org/wgbh/pages/frontline/shows/jefferson/cron/1868randall.html
(3) Jefferson's blood. Retrieved December 14, 2016, from http://www.pbs.org/wgbh/pages/frontline/shows/jefferson/true/Retrieved December 14, 2016, from http://www.usnews.com/usnews/issue/981109/9tom.htm
(4) Is it true? - A Primer on Jefferson Dna. Retrieved December 14, 2016, from http://www.pbs.org/wgbh/pages/frontline/shows/jefferson/true/primer.html Retrieved December 14, 2016, from https://www.insidehighered.com/sites/default/server_files/styles/large/public/media/Jefferson 2.jpg?itok=-xSGPd3Z

Thomas Paine: The Original Emancipator
Hitchens, C. (1996). Triumvirate of rationalism: Thomas Paine, Thomas Jefferson, and George Orwell - kindle edition by Christopher Hitchens. Politics & social sciences kindle eBooks @ Amazon.Com. Retrieved December 14, 2016, from Amazon.com: Kindle Store, https://www.amazon.com/dp/B01MDJVFDS/ref=docs-os-doi_0

Fidel Castro is defended
(1) Goldman, D. (2016, December 14). Fidel Castro's mass murder by the numbers. Retrieved December 14, 2016, from https://pjmedia.com/spengler/2016/11/28/fidel-castros-mass-murder-by-the-numbers/
(2) Gomez, H. L. (2012, May 2). Fidel Castro's greatest atrocities and crimes - introduction | Babalú Blog. Retrieved December 14, 2016, from Babalú Blog, http://babalublog.com/fidel-castros-greatest-atrocities-and-crimes/
(3) Military units to aid production (2016). . In Wikipedia. Retrieved from https://plaza.en.wikipedia.org/wiki/Military_Units_to_Aid_Production
(4) http://plaza.ufl.edu/lillian.guerra/pdfs/lillian-guerra-social-history.pdf
(5) Kirchick, J. (2016, November 27). Fidel Castro's horrific record on Gay Rights. Retrieved December 14, 2016, from world, http://www.thedailybeast.com/articles/2016/11/27/don-t-forget-fidel-castro-s-brutal-oppression-of-gay-people.html
(6) Capitulo Unico - Cuba 1967a. Retrieved December 14, 2016, from http://www.cidh.org/countryrep/cuba67sp/cap.1a.htm Retrieved December 14, 2016, from http://www.cidh.org/countryrep/cuba67sp/cap.1a.ht

December

Fact Checking – The Newest Trend
(1) Adams, C. (2016, December 5). Man opens fire in D.C. Restaurant while looking into fake news story about Hillary Clinton: Cops. Retrieved December 14, 2016, from http://people.com/crime/man-opens-fire-in-d-c-restaurant-while-self-investigating-fake-news-story-about-hillary-clinton/
(2) Pizzagate (conspiracy theory) (2016). . In Wikipedia. Retrieved from https://en.wikipedia.org/wiki/Pizzagate_(conspiracy_theory)

The Republic [Abridged Book Review]

Plato and Griffith, T. (2000) Plato: The republic. Edited by G. R. F. Ferrari. Cambridge: Cambridge University Press.

What is Populism?

(1) The rise (and fall) of the populist party (no date) Available at:
https://d2ct263enury6r.cloudfront.net/1JzlH9P3EAzIB4pjipqrtYQx3ZNk9VME1YmvIDE5fsWkT
w5U.pdf (Accessed: 16 December 2016).
(2) Is Donald Trump a populist? (2016) Available at: http://www.economist.com/blogs/economist-explains/2016/07/economist-explains-0 (Accessed: 16 December 2016).
(3) The Populist Party"; "The Election of 1896"; "William Jennings Bryan".American History. ABC-CLIO
Schools Subscription Web Sites. 20 January 2006<http://www.americanhistory.abc-clio.com>.

Russian Hack Investigation

(1) Bastasch, M. (2016) 'Racist DNC Email flagrantly makes fun of black woman's name', .
(2) Shear, M.D. and Rosenberg, M. (2016) 'Released Emails suggest the D.N.C. Derided the Sanders
campaign', Politics, .
(3) Entous, A. and Nakashima, E. (2016) FBI in agreement with CIA that Russia aimed to help trump win
white house. Available at: https://www.washingtonpost.com/politics/clinton-blames-putins-personal-grudge-against-her-for-election-interference/2016/12/16/12f36250-c3be-11e6-8422-eac61c0ef74d_story.html?utm_term=.09297cbafd06 (Accessed: 19 December 2016).
(4) Logan, B. (2016) Top US intelligence agency hints electoral college briefing on Russian hacking won't
happen anytime soon. Available at: http://www.businessinsider.com/electoral-college-briefing-russian-hacking-dni-2016-12 (Accessed: 19 December 2016).
(5) "TV-Novosti"AutonomousNonprofitOrganization (2016) WikiLeaks calls on Obama to submit proof of
Russian hacking for verification. Available at: https://www.rt.com/usa/370567-wikileaks-obama-russian-hacking-docs/ (Accessed: 19 December 2016).
(6) Smith-Spark, L. (2016) Russia challenges US to prove campaign hacking claims or shut up. Available
at: http://www.cnn.com/2016/12/16/europe/russia-us-hacking-claims-peskov/ (Accessed: 19
December 2016).

www.ingramcontent.com/pod-product-compliance
Lightning Source LLC
Chambersburg PA
CBHW051413280526
45785CB00003B/1054